house

AUSTRALIAN
HOUSE
&GARDEN

house

...for everyone who loves their home

ACPbooks

a new way of living

Each of us lives in some sort of house. It may be a renovated terrace in the hub of the inner city, or a bungalow in the sprawling suburbs. It may be a one-room apartment high in the sky or, if you're lucky, an extravagant estate in the calm of the country. Wherever you live, your home is a very important place. A house means shelter, a house means warmth, a house hopefully means happiness with other special people, and a house often becomes our only true vehicle for personal expression. Over a lifetime, a house also soaks up a good deal of our hard-earned money so it's very important to get it right. HOUSE is about just that — a fast track to creating your perfect space for living life, cooking, eating, entertaining, playing with the kids, relaxing, sleeping, bathing and even working...

This living space epitomises the more casual approach to room arrangement and decoration in modern homes. There are separate 'zones' for conversation and dining (either indoors or out), and the action takes place in full view of the cook.

living

When you're a modern person living at today's pace — fast and furious — the concept of relaxation involves more than just slowing down. Relaxation is all about being around your family; people who understand you. It's about turning the mobile phone off and the answering machine on. The living room is the place where you kick back and chill out. It embraces everything you need to relax and bring balance to a hectic lifestyle. Today's living space offers a place for informal interaction with family and friends, a vehicle for personal expression in decorating and, most importantly, a room in which to do your own thing and restore life's harmony.

living zones

In days gone by the lounge room, as it was commonly called, had a clearly defined function: it was the 'best' room in the house, a place for polite conversation where guests were entertained and children were seen but not heard. Today the lounge room has become the living space, and that's exactly what it's used for – living. As children and adults mix in this area, it makes sense to build in a degree of flexibility. Take into account toddlers' play, teenagers' study and partying as well as zones for more passive activities and areas devoted to casual entertaining. But no matter how many zones your living room has, the emphasis is on relaxation. For some this means time alone, while for others it means togetherness.

1. COMFORT

The comfort zone in many homes is in front of the fireplace or heater in winter, and cooling fan or appealing leafy green or water view in summer. The physical cosiness should be supplemented with tactile warmth: knitted throws and soft fabrics on chairs and cushions, and a thick plush rug under bare toes, for instance. Old-fashioned values of warmth and comfort are intrinsic in this new-fashioned living space, with its focus on the open hearth. But in summer, the space welcomes in soft breezes from the garden.

2. ENTERTAINING

When all is said and done, living rooms are essentially for grown-ups; they're just shared with the kids. It's important to have a space that will come up trumps for a party, where children's toys can be quickly stashed away and furniture rearranged to create a place for guests. The zone should also accommodate casual seating, such as stackable chairs, as well as a sumptuous sofa. Side tables can be pushed together to hold buffet food and a console can serve as a bar. The fabulous lounging corner shown here features Knoll Platner glass-topped tables-cum-cushioned stools.

3. EATING

There was a time when eating was forbidden in the lounge room, but today's modern living space actively encourages it. Eating is one of the things we do to relax, and eating is also part of entertaining. There can be several zones demarcated for casual eating, from the coffee table to the outdoor deck. Children will need to know they can share the space, but on adults' terms. The drinks cabinet should be lockable and out of bounds. This open-sided deck extends the home's living space for alfresco dining.

4. READING

One of the most important elements of a modern living space is a quiet zone, a corner by a window or under a skylight specifically dedicated as a place for reading. You can segregate this area with a screen or by using the back of a sofa as a divider. This is a place for peaceful reflection – definitely out of bounds for the television. An easy chair or recliner with footstool, a reading lamp and small side table for books make things comfortable. Here, quiet luxury takes on a modern manner, with chenille damask and glove-like suede on the cushions.

5. INDOOR/OUTDOOR

Blurring the boundaries between indoors and out allows you extra room to entertain. It's especially good for a multi-generation party as guests, young and old, can feel comfortable in their own space.

6. PLAY

If you share your life with children and pets, you have to expect they'll share your living space. If there is no separate family room or playroom (or even if there is), it's important to have a child-friendly area in the living room reserved for adult/child interaction. This family moved back the furniture to create plenty of floor space to sprawl out and read.

7. CONVERSATION

A living room's structure is based around the furniture grouping. After all, the sofa is where you sit down and talk. Even with so many other activities going on, conversation is still to be encouraged and enjoyed. Arranging the primary seating around a focal point like a fireplace or big picture window (but not the television set or stereo) is a great way to draw people into the space. There is no distinct division between living, dining and kitchen in this house, but the sofa easily defines the place for conversation.

8. WATCHING TV/ LISTENING TO MUSIC

The television seems to have found a permanent place in the living room. It's often turned on unconsciously, in much the same way a radio used to be. To minimise its intrusion, integrate the set into a cabinet or shelving. Position some seating directly in front so you can watch it without craning your neck. For music appreciation, identify an area away from traffic, where you can sit and relax. In this open-plan living room, a small, discreet television on castors allows more flexibility; it can be moved around so the 'viewing zone' moves with it.

9. DISPLAY

Having somewhere to stash and stow the clutter a family generates is crucial. A central location for children's toys, videos and magazines is useful, but it's not all about hiding things away. Having a place for displaying things that give personal pleasure, such as framed artworks, family photos and beautiful books, is vitally important. A living room without these things is a space without soul. Strike a balance by confining your collections to purpose-built shelves and keep the ragtag clutter at bay in roll-out storage bins, a chest or dresser. Display niches were created in this room to show off art glass and ceramics.

livingstyle

Few memorable living spaces are created overnight. One of the reasons for this is that our lives don't stand still, therefore our rooms should evolve as we do. There will be many different things to influence your style as you venture along your particular decorating path. But remember, living rooms are to be lived in by everyone. It is where you entertain, relax, have fun. It's also where you meet your children on common ground, so there's a true sense of family and community. Spaces may even flow to the outdoors. Choose a decorating style to suit all roles. Design ideas gleaned from books, magazines and the homes you see around you are a great way to begin the creative process. Adapt them to suit the way you live.

1. MILAN CHIC

Polished and contemporary, this style typifies a European sensibility in the way compact living spaces are designed. Customised built-in joinery and refined architectural detailing give it its signature. There is a strong use of wood, particularly oak. Fabrics are soft and somewhat sexy, yet technically state-of-the-art. Seating is structured, functional and often multi-purpose. The colours are subtle, hinging on variations of light and shade to make an impact. The apartment here has a sophisticated international air and a sense of order, but the atmosphere is wonderfully warm and inviting.

2. HIP CLASSIC

Classicism with an edge is how you would describe this style. Artistic licence allows a mix of old and new, as long as the modern pieces have character. Bold colour takes a back seat and lush creams and chalky whites come to the fore. Antique pieces are re-covered in modern fabrics. Floors, whether carpet or stone, are pale. Beautiful cushions and Chinoiserie influences in accessories add classic touches. Artworks are likely to be framed ceremonial prints, calligraphy or a series of botanical prints. The soft rich cream palette in this room is ideal for playing up a collection of blue-and-white porcelain and oriental design elements.

3. ART LOVER

For this living style you want clean, bright surfaces to pick up on the clarity of colour in artworks. White walls are fine but many paintings and sculptures do look quite remarkable against robust colour. Furniture can be a mix of old and new with an emphasis on comfort rather than designer status. This vibrant family room is alive with colour and originality. A painted screen gives clout to a corner while a sectional sofa is positioned to bring intimacy.

4. COMMUNITY

Even minimalists have children eventually (or friends with kids), and that means the introduction of ample storage and family-friendly surfaces that extend to a dining area and kitchen. This casual 'family' style is soft-edge, as opposed to hard-edge contemporary, and based around comfort and convenience. It allows for some clutter and plenty of washable wall space for artworks, and places to put the television and stereo gear. Furniture is an eclectic mix centred around a modern, floor-hugging sofa and large, low coffee table which can be used for informal meals.

5. CITYSCAPE

Rich colour, plush textures, exotic veneers and elegant furniture enforce the glamour of this style. The influence is heavily New York and the view is the calling card. It's a decorator style that is inspirational by day, dramatic by night. When avid furniture collectors moved from their house to this ritzy apartment with its dazzling city skyline, they decided to put the more conservative pieces into storage and focus on the Art Deco which forms the backbone to this timeless style.

livingstyle

6. CITY TO SURF
This look captures the essence of the coast with its calming colours and cool surfaces, but is sophisticated enough for any city slicker. There's nothing quaint or even beachy here. Its reference to the coast is found in principles of light, space and cross-ventilation. Unpretentious surfaces deal with the daily wear and tear of indoor/outdoor living. Here, custom-designed furniture in laminate and Zincalume and a floor of polished concrete allow for maximum durability.

7. EURO PROVINCIAL
This is not the chicken-at-the-door Provençal style but something incredibly more chic and refined. Here, traditional features such as ironwork, wicker, stone and wood may mingle with chandeliers and elegant light fittings, as well as imposing mirrors and exquisite fabrics like leather, velvet and organza. Rather than draw attention away from the fabrics and accessories, a neutral scheme harmonises with them. This living room opens its doors to the garden, allowing the provincial theme to extend its reach.

8. MINIMALIST
This style is all about space, light and absolutely no superfluous detail. Pure white dominates, though minimalism doesn't always mean modern and it certainly doesn't mean an empty room. It creates the ambience to showcase designer furniture and accessories. But forget this style if you have kids – children need to make a mess, so this look isn't practical for a family home. The designer of this living room has chosen brilliant white as a background to accentuate an impressive collection of iconic designer furniture. Windows are left unadorned to reveal their intrinsic shape.

9. TRAVELLER

There is unending pleasure in a room that surrounds you with memories of favourite travels. Paintings or textiles bought on holiday become the inspiration for a colour scheme. Ethnic artefacts are lived with, not merely looked at. In this apartment, a core collection of rugs, books, artworks and furniture from around the world sets the scene. The Le Corbusier seats are at home with New Guinea masks, 1950s Burmese chairs, a sugar-cane crusher used as a side table, Balinese textiles and photographic art.

10. RETRO

This urban style looks to the mid-20th century Modernists for inspiration. The mood is uncluttered, with pattern that is restrained yet striking. Furniture emphasises sculptural, organic forms, making the most of semi-industrial materials such as steel, glass and light plywood. Replicating the 'modern' look of the early 1950s, which focused attention on new-age materials like polished chrome, this setting includes a stainless-steel coffee table, reconditioned metal locker and chrome chairs with an abstract 1950s print.

11. FUNKY

This is a courageous decorating style relying on a confident hand with colour and pattern. This Pop look is easy to achieve if you can find appropriate fabrics to re-cover traditional chairs or sofas. Spherical and elliptical shapes are important, as is coloured glass. The living room in this tiny terrace house gets a cardio-funk work-out in brilliant colour and outrageous patterning. An original fireplace has been given a splash of red, echoing the vivid, arty fabrics covering the sofa and chair. The bright colour is used only as an accent, which is the reason why this works so well.

10

11

livingcolour

Working out colours for your home's living space requires a careful strategy. It's an area with competing high-energy and relaxing zones, used by children and adults, and you need a scheme that bridges these differences. But whatever colours you choose, both you and your family should love them. No amount of colour theory will persuade a shy person to surround themselves with magenta walls. And if a room is on a home's shady side, it's madness to paint it stark white or ice blue as these will accentuate its coolness. Existing furnishings, particularly the floor, will also determine your choice. But there are basic colour laws and when you understand how and why these fundamentals work, choosing hues becomes so easy.

1. NEUTRALS WITH A WARM ACCENT COLOUR

This scheme is based on a neutral palette of whites, beige, wood tones and grey, with a splash of hot colour to accent. The treatment of colour in this apartment adds spatial interest while emphasising a play of light and shadow. Here, texture works hand in hand with the colour palette.

2. MONOCHROMATIC

Based around one colour, in this case several shades and tints of blue, this monochromatic scheme delivers a dramatic, memorable effect. A highlight of grey-blue Colourstone acts as a footpath, leading from the kitchen to the table. Echoing the span of a blue-painted bulkhead above, it brings a sense of movement to the space.

3. PRIMARY COLOUR

Yellow is the colour of the sun and it brings warmth and happiness to a room. It is a whimsical colour and takes the seriousness out of spare, minimalist spaces where white predominates. It also bridges the generation gap; children love it as do adults, making it a particularly good choice for a family living space.

4. TRIADIC COLOURS

A triadic scheme uses three colours equidistant from each other on the colour wheel (see page 24). The scheme here features red, blue and yellow. The brilliance is toned down with a soft yellow that works as a background to the more vibrant accents.

5. NEUTRALS

This palette of soft earthy neutrals crosses the boundaries of style. It is appealing as a background to both classic and contemporary design and allows furniture and artworks to be shown to their best effect. Subtle and sophisticated, this scheme can be updated in later years as the lifestyle and colour preferences of a family changes.

6. COMPLEMENTARY WITH TERTIARY COLOURS

This sophisticated colour scheme balances a cool light tone with a warm, dark colour and a fresh sweep of neutrals. The maroon used on the fireplace surround creates a visual trick that makes it appear to advance and 'float' against the pale green wall.

livingcolour

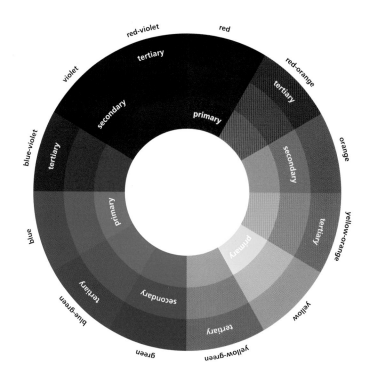

1. Cushions introduce a gentle splash of colour to a cream sofa.
2. Pale tones and curvy shapes are highlighted when set against dark aubergine walls.
3. Artworks add dynamic colour and character to a living space.

USING A COLOUR WHEEL

A colour wheel is an incredibly useful tool for choosing colours. Red, yellow and blue are the three primary colours and they are placed equidistant from each other on the wheel. In between those are the secondary colours – green, orange and purple – which are mixes of two of the three primaries. In between those again are the tertiary colours (like olive and burgundy) which are mixes of two of the three secondary colours. As the colours fan out on the wheel, it's easy to see how they relate, which ones contrast and which ones are cool- or warm-based.

Choose colours from the opposite sides of the wheel, for instance blue and orange, and you have a balanced, 'complementary' colour scheme. Select colours that sit side by side, such as blue and green, or orange and yellow, and you create a 'related' scheme. Divide the wheel in half through the axis of yellow-green and red-violet, and you separate the cool from the warm colours. Warm schemes centre on orange; cool schemes on blue.

SUIT YOUR LIFESTYLE

How you live influences your colour choice. If young children are rampaging around you'll want a practical scheme with some primaries; those with grown-up children may find pleasure in having a sophisticated scheme of neutrals.

How you use the space, whether casually or formally, also makes a difference. Casual colours tend to be the mid-tone hues, for example terracotta or french blue. Darker, saturated colours such as red, burgundy, navy or aubergine have a formality that suits the dining zone.

OPEN-PLAN SCHEMES

In open-plan areas, design your scheme around one main colour with at least two darker accents. A complementary scheme of warm and cool colours or an accented neutral scheme are good choices.

Where there is a dining area, position the table near a wall you can paint as a feature in a warm colour, such as burnt orange. Orange is said to stimulate the appetite and is more formal than terracotta which, in fact, could be taken into the kitchen where the action is more casual.

Target the relaxing zone, around the sofas, with a cool colour such as steely blue. Consider, too, blurring the boundaries between indoors and out by echoing an interior colour on an adjoining exterior wall. This will help visually expand the living and entertaining space.

livingstorage

While no place for serious relaxing and living can ever be consistently tidy – children regularly up-end Lego boxes and bookworms create teetering piles of tomes – everyday detritus can soon take over if it doesn't have a place to call home. A logical, disciplined approach to storage need not be at odds with the pursuit of relaxation. Knowing that things have an allocated niche will simplify the process of clearing up and leave surfaces and corners clutter-free. Whether you opt for freestanding or built-in storage will depend, in part, on how long you plan to stay in your home, but choose the storage that suits you best.

1. A low storage unit slots neatly behind a sofa to screen its blank upholstered back. The unit's raised-off-the-floor design, slender legs and white and glass finishes reflect the contemporary mood of the living space.
2. Set against a feature wall, an antique armoire creates a magnificent focal point in a room of natural textures and Asian influences. It has been modified to discreetly house the television and hi-fi.

BUILT-IN OR NOT?

The serene effects of a minimalist interior owe much to clever concealed storage, which generally comes with a hefty price-tag. But it's true that well-designed built-ins can add to the value and appeal of your home. The downside is that you can't take them with you when you leave. In any case, where a wide range of things needs to be housed, custom-built storage is often the best solution.

Start by assessing a room for its potential for built-in storage or housing large freestanding pieces such as an armoire or dresser. While storage should always complement the existing bones of a space, it can also disguise awkward architectural configurations. A tall, slim unit, for instance, can play up the verticals in a low-ceilinged space, while lofty rooms can take floor-to-ceiling storage without it being overbearing.

Built-ins that line a wall and continue above and around a doorway give a pleasing sense of intimacy, while alcoves on either side of a chimney are crying out for open shelves or cupboards.

Seating built into bay windows or alcoves offers great potential for storage, with drawers beneath the seat being less disruptive than a lift-top design. In particularly tight spaces, consider drawers that slot into the wall cavity. Where space permits, you could even put in a false wall to accommodate built-in storage.

An arrangement of alcoves can break the monotony of a long sweep of wall and provide display space. To heighten the impact of the display, include internal accent lighting or paint the alcove interiors in feature colours.

Modular furniture is a hybrid of freestanding and built-in storage, and gives you the freedom to assemble units into various configurations, add in more later, or pull the whole lot down and start again. It's particularly popular for housing audio and video gear. But as with any big-volume storage area, try to balance the amount of open shelving and cupboard doors so the end result looks good.

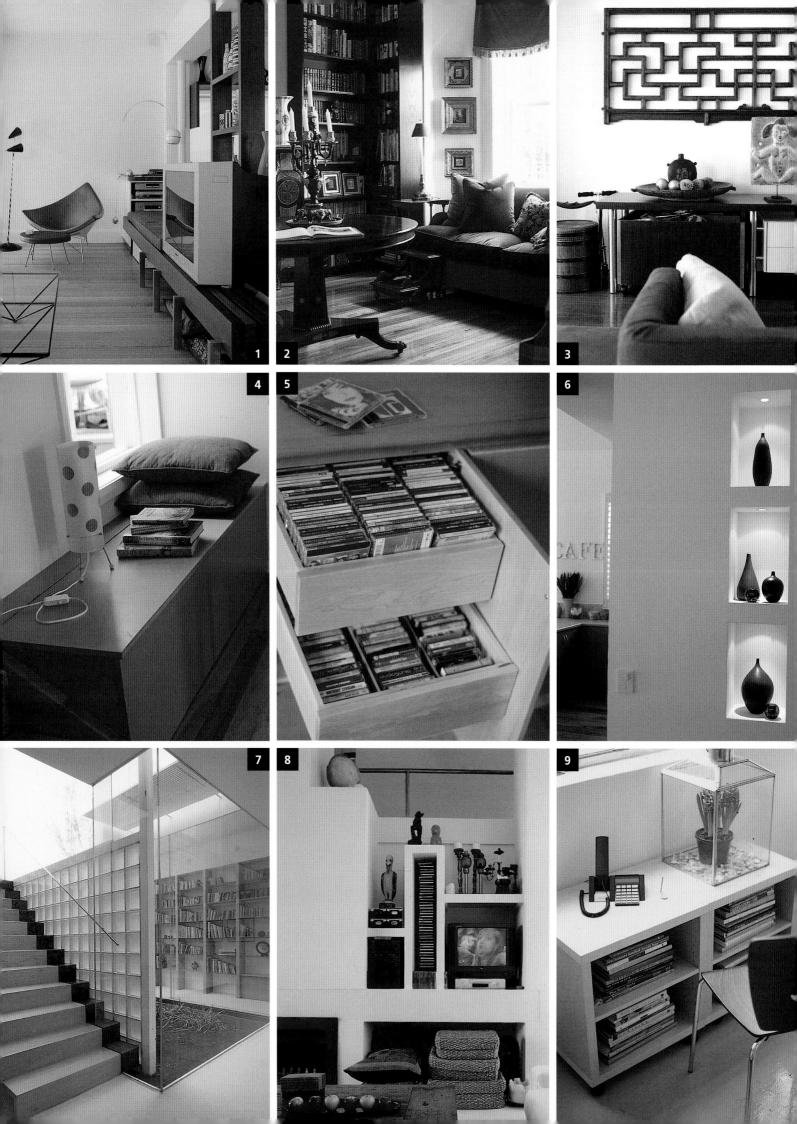

1. Jarrah shelves divide the kitchen from the living areas, while keeping the space open to the views, light and breezes. A slatted bench serves as both a shelf for the television and storage for cushions; one end is cushioned for seating.

2. Custom-built shelves in a dark wood veneer lend appropriate seriousness for a library of classic style. The corner arrangement makes for an efficient use of space, without dominating the room.

3. Storage cubes fitted with castors and integrated into a freestanding modular unit make light work of tidying up children's clutter in the family room and kitchen.

4. A built-in chest, made of economical particle board, provides a place for long-term storage in a compact room.

5. A Canadian rock-maple cupboard fitted with shelves keeps cassettes and CDs out of sight but within easy reach.

6. Display alcoves break up a wall dividing the kitchen from the living area, and frame a collection of glass and ceramics. The alcoves are fitted with recessed downlighting to show off the pieces to best effect.

7. Blond timber and glass give a wall of shelving a lightness of touch, befitting the tranquillity of a living space arranged around a pond.

8. A space adjacent to the chimney breast is divided into compartments to store audio-visual equipment and display a collection of artefacts. A deep alcove at the base, one of a pair, stows firewood at the rear and floor cushions for lounging next to the fire. Stacked lidded baskets store videotapes.

9. Two storage units on castors are pushed together to make a phone table. Separated, they're perfect bedside tables.

10. Jaunty red doors hide clutter unworthy of display in a set of otherwise open shelves.

10

STORAGE IDEAS

● Shelving is best treated so that visually it becomes part of the wall.

● Edging or beading fixed along the front and sides of shelves gives them solidity, and painting them the same colour as the wall creates unity.

● Pigeonhole shelves are great for storing magazines, books and videos.

● A unit that combines a cupboard and shelves provides space to hide clutter and also to display objects.

● Store breakables and delicate items above child height, and child-friendly or heavy items on the lower shelves.

● Deep shelving, as well as cupboards, benefits from a little light so you can see what's inside. Consider recessing strip lighting behind shelf beading.

● Maximise your storage with furniture that does double duty: an ottoman with a lift-top or a coffee table with shelves for magazines and drawers for CDs.

● Storage units on castors can be pushed together to zone off an open space, while a decorative folding screen can section off a corner for stowing large, awkward items such as golf clubs or skis.

● Include some less structured storage to allow for a quick tidy-up or to ease the transformation from kids' play area to adult space at the day's end. Large baskets, screens and alcoves fitted with a drop of fabric allow for rapid clear-ups.

● As televisions, videos, hi-fi and computers radiate heat, their storage areas need to be well ventilated. Have a cable-management system set up to make sense of a tangle of wires.

● To avoid the television becoming a focus, store it behind cupboard doors.

● Speakers are best secured off the floor and fronted with steel mesh doors if they are to be stored out of sight.

● Make sure bookshelves are securely attached to structurally sound walls, and have support brackets at sufficient intervals for the weight of the books.

● Floors supporting heavy freestanding book storage should be load-bearing.

living walls&floors

Although the living area's focus is on relaxation, much of the time it's a hive of activity – and that means a hard slog for surfaces. Floors and walls have to be durable enough to withstand this wear and tear. They should be able to cope with a constant stream of human traffic, while also contributing to the room's comfortable mood. If the living area extends to the outdoors, there's yet another choice: do you want to make a match with the outdoor 'room' to unify the space, or go for a clever contrast?

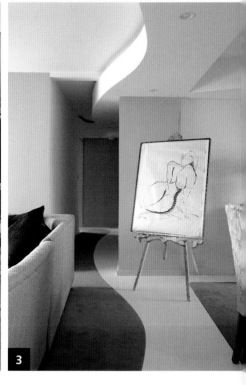

WALLS

It's amazing the daily grime that ends up on living room walls when there's a growing family around. To combat this, treat walls with a washable surface. Choose a semi-sheen, washable paint, or if you are using wallpaper, one with a wipeable finish. Textured papers and wood panelling on the wall also defuse the damage potential to busy living areas.

PRACTICAL FLOORS

Living room floors must be tough enough to take heavy foot traffic and easy to clean, but also easy to live with.

Carpet is warm, soft and not as damaging to toddlers when they take a tumble. Most importantly, it muffles sound. For living areas, you should choose a carpet with a stain-resistant finish or a pattern built for camouflage to cope with spills.

Sisal and coir are popular, but coir is scratchy on babies' knees, and both stain and show water marks unless treated.

Timber floors look chic and are often preferred by people with allergies, as they're easier to clean than other flooring. But a timber floor can be noisy, so add a few rugs with non-slip backings for extra hush.

Tile, stone or concrete floors can extend outside or into the kitchen to pull together a space. They're ideal for an adult household (kids prefer to sprawl on softer surfaces) and easy to clean, but they can be cold in winter and amplify sound. Putting rugs down will keep noise under control, however, and underfloor heating will take off the cool edge in winter.

1. With a courtyard adjacent, this room benefits from commercial-grade vinyl tiles to help tackle the foot traffic.
2. Wood makes a clean backdrop to retro furnishings. The owners unified their collection of 1950s chairs by covering them all in red fabric.
3. Carpet and limestone marry well in this apartment, setting a colour scheme that's also seen on the walls. The curve repeats the line of the bulkhead above.
4. This super glossy floor is actually concrete. It was diamond ground to an almost smooth finish, given a base coat of epoxy with added grey, then a second coat tinted with green.

SOFT FLOORS
CARPET

Carpet can be made of wool or synthetic fibres, or a blend. Combinations of 80 per cent wool and 20 per cent nylon, or 40 per cent wool and 60 per cent acrylic, make a good, all-purpose carpet. Remember, wool and wool-blend carpets require moth protection. And if you want your carpet to look good for longer, invest in a quality underlay. Usually the label tells you if a carpet is suited to light, medium or heavy domestic use. Light-use carpets are good for bedrooms and some living areas; medium-use suit living areas, family rooms and kids' bedrooms; and heavy-use can cope with busy family rooms, stairs, hallways and entrances. The type of pile gives a carpet its distinct look and also affects its durability.

Loop pile A continuous row of loops makes a hard-wearing surface and minimises tracking from footprints.

Cut pile Also called velour pile, yarns are sheared to produce a smooth finish. It looks luxurious but is prone to shading.

Hard-twist cut pile Also called frise cut pile, the yarns are cut and tightly twisted, then heat set. It's very hard-wearing and less prone to shedding.

Cut-and-loop pile Some yarns are cut and others left as loops to create patterns.

Shag pile This is cut longer than cut pile and has a sensuous feel, but is best in bedrooms and light-traffic areas.

NATURAL FIBRE FLOORCOVERINGS

Natural fibre floorcoverings usually have a latex backing and can be made into rugs or laid wall-to-wall. But they hate the wet: coir expands and buckles and sisal shrinks if they get soaked. Except for seagrass, all need stain protection.

Coir This coconut-husk fibre is durable but prickly. It's great for heavy-traffic areas but a little harsh for bedrooms.

Sisal Made from the agave plant, sisal is tough enough to take heavy traffic but is much kinder on feet than coir.

Jute Softer than coir or sisal but also less durable. It won't stand up to heavy wear.

Seagrass Cheap and tough, seagrass doesn't stain like other natural fibres. You should vacuum these floors regularly, but never wash or shampoo them.

WOOD FLOORS

Wood is hard-wearing and looks better the older it gets. It's laid mostly as tongue-and-groove boards or parquetry. Whether it's stained or not, all wood should be sealed. Polyurethane, varnish, alkyd resin sealant or natural resin or oil can all be used. However all sealants wear off eventually and must be reapplied. Less expensive than wood is laminate flooring, a plastic-coated wood veneer (cork veneer is also available) glued to plywood. Sold in tongue-and-groove pieces, it's laid over an existing floor. It's easy to clean and almost stainproof.

1. This scheme contrasts polished timber and stone, with the timber laid to direct the eye outdoors. Stone tiles, the same as those used outside, delineate the conversation area.

2. Sliding glass doors remove the barrier between indoors and out in this family home. A blackbutt timber floor, lightened with a limewash finish, extends through the living and kitchen areas. Its muted colours make a subtle contrast to charcoal hued pavers used in the courtyard.

It's the pile that gives a carpet its distinctive look. Shown are: **3.** Shag pile. **4.** Hard-twist cut pile. **5.** Cut pile. **6.** Textured loop pile. **7.** Level loop pile.

2

3   4   5   6   7

IN WHAT ORDER SHOULD YOU PAINT A ROOM?

1. First coat on the ceiling and the cornice.
2. First coat on the walls.
3. Second coat on the ceiling and cornice.
4. First coat or undercoat (if using a gloss paint) on timber trims (skirtings, windows, doors, etc). Once dry, sand back lightly.
5. Second coat on walls.
6. Final coat on timber trims.
7. If the floor is being varnished, then do it as the final thing.

livinglighting&windows

Windows are your home's eyes to the world and, in a living space, they are usually an important part of the architecture. Both sunlight and artificial lighting have to be considered when you're figuring out a lighting plan. Before you formalise the plan, look at what your family actually does in the living area. Do they watch television or do cross-stitch? The more activities, the more flexible your lighting must be.

1

2

3

A PRACTICAL LIGHTING PLAN

- Have a mix of ambient and task lighting. Whether downlights, pendants or uplighters, your ambient lighting should be fitted with a dimmer switch.
- Use several different circuits with dimmer switches. That way, you can choose which lights you dim.
- Task lighting doesn't have to be fixed. It can be as simple as a table lamp next to a chair or a floor lamp you can angle to throw light where it's required. Lamps are also good for illuminating dark corners.
- Pale walls reflect light and dark walls absorb it. Don't fit too-powerful bulbs on uplighters against a pale wall or you'll make a giant reflector.

LIGHTING

To work successfully, a living area needs a variety of lighting: a good level of ambient or background light and task lighting that can be directed where it's needed, especially for reading or undertaking fine work. Accent lighting (directional spotlights or low-voltage picture lights) can draw attention to a treasured object.

Try to have a balanced level of ambient (background) light. Instead of a single pendant light, which can cast shadows, use a series of downlights or a couple of uplighters on the walls – and fit them with a dimmer switch so you can turn down the glow when you're relaxing or watching the television.

1. Frameless laminated glass welcomes in the blue horizon at a beachside home.
2. Glass walls, with a pivot door, make the courtyard an extension of the living area in this inner-city house. The high boundary walls outside mean privacy isn't an issue.
3. This wall of sleek, metal-framed pivot doors lets through cooling breezes.
4. A row of sky windows and a pool outside play light across panels of colour-backed glass in this dining area. The light show changes through the day.

livinglighting&windows

WINDOWS

As living areas have been opened to the outdoors, traditional windows have been replaced by sliding and concertina doors, effectively creating walls of glass.

More glass, however, means more sun, more heat and also more ultraviolet (UV) radiation, which over time fades paint, fabrics, furnishings and artworks.

Standard 3mm thick window glass lets through 70 per cent of UV, but it's easy to counteract by fitting sunscreens, blinds or curtains, or by using laminated glass which cuts out up to 99 per cent of UV.

Curtains and blinds also combat heat loss – windows let out up to 25 per cent of the heat in an uninsulated home. To keep a room snug, extend curtains or blinds at least 10cm beyond the edge of the window, finish them 1cm to 2cm off the floor, and extend them above the window – the usual distance is 15cm.

LIGHTING BASICS
LIGHTING USES

There are three categories of lighting:

Ambient light This is the general, overall lighting in a room. It's usually provided by a central light, although using several sources of light, for example, a series of downlights, creates less shadowing than having one bulb in the middle of the room. Adding a dimmer means you can change the atmosphere, for example reducing the background light for a candlelit dinner or to watch television.

Task lighting This is concentrated lighting that illuminates one area brightly. Spotlights, low-voltage halogen lights or fluorescent tubes fitted above benches are all effective in getting good light onto work surfaces.

Accent lighting This is low-level, focused light targeted at a particular feature, such as a painting. But in most homes, if the ambient and task lighting are right, there's little need for accent lighting. Of course, if you do have a Picasso, by all means show it off.

TYPES OF LIGHT

Natural light Sunlight is inviting, doesn't distort colour and is the whitest, purest light known. However in summer sunlight also means heat, so don't overdo skylights and windows without adequate shading.

Tungsten The familiar domestic incandescent bulb is easily dimmable and produces a warm light that's flattering to skin tones. The minuses are poor energy efficiency and a short lifespan (1000 hours average). Although ordinary bulbs throw a dispersed light, internally silvered reflector bulbs can be used to give a directional beam.

Tungsten-halogen Commonly called halogen bulbs, these use a tungsten filament inside a bulb with halogen gas. They produce a concentrated, bright white light, and put out the same amount of light as ordinary tungsten bulbs at a lower voltage and a smaller size. They're the most versatile lights, as they can be used for either ambient or task lighting and can be used with a dimmer. They'll last for up to 3000 hours, but run hotter than tungsten bulbs. This extra heat should be dispersed with dichroic reflectors and heatproof mountings. Low-voltage bulbs (12 volts or less) must be used in conjunction with a transformer to reduce the mains voltage.

Fluorescent This produces light by passing electricity through argon or krypton gas in a tube and exciting phosphorescing coating on the glass. Fluorescents come as straight or circular tubes or as long-life bulbs (compact fluorescents). Fluorescents are cheap to run (about one-tenth the cost of incandescents) and last about 8000 hours. The drawbacks are that they can't be used with a standard dimmer (you'll need extra electronic ballasts) and there's a disposal problem because of the toxic chemicals they contain.

1. During the day, a lofty void pulls sunlight into the core of this narrow townhouse. At night, carefully positioned spotlights focus on designer features. A bank of downlights bounce their gleam off the polished concrete floor for even background lighting.
2. This is the ultimate indoor/outdoor transition space. Located in an iconic building, it has a glass louvre facade that can be adjusted to catch the harbour breeze. There are also roller blinds for added shade.
3. Sliding glass doors open to a deep terrace in this bayside home and allow for good cross-ventilation. Roller blinds of sunscreen fabric (PVC-coated woven fibreglass) tame the heat and glare on hot days.
4. Sensibly placed lamps deliver a boost of brightness where it's needed in this harbourside apartment. Ambient light levels are reasonably subdued so as not to detract from the impressive view.

livingfurniture

With the modern penchant for lighter, brighter, more open living spaces, you need less formal furniture but more carefully chosen pieces. To make the living space flexible enough to cope with a number of different functions, choose multi-purpose, portable designs and modular furniture that can be rearranged and added to as the family grows and changes and budgets hopefully expand.

1

2

3

A CASUAL APPROACH

As lifestyles have become more casual, so too has the furniture. Gone are the days of the matching three-piece suite; today, the style is for more flexible, informal combinations of sofas, ottomans and chairs.

The more relaxed you get, the closer to the floor you go. The look now is for low-slung furniture which replaces the high, upright seating associated with the formal drawing rooms of years past.

This informality is taken to the extreme in the lounging lifestyles of young urban apartment dwellers. The culture of lying back and relaxing on the floor has given birth to furniture that is a hybrid of the sofa and bed – the living platform – carpet-skimming in height and made of modular

elements such as swivelling tabletops and pull-out drawers, providing an arena to eat and work as well as lounge.

In keeping with modern airy spaces, sofas and coffee tables are increasingly raised off the floor on slimline legs to give the appearance of lightness. But this isn't a hard-and-fast rule: in truly flexible living spaces, it's not clean-lined legs but lockable castors that are preferred.

As the ultimate multi-functional piece of furniture, ottomans are a modern living essential, providing storage, footrest, seating and table all in one.

Mixing sofas and chairs also gives flexibility. For instance, a grouping of a sofa and two chairs is more adaptable in an arrangement than two sofas.

1. Raised off the floor on polished metal legs, this sofa attains a lightness of being without compromising on comfort. The matching oatmeal upholstery of the sofa and ottoman creates harmony.
2. Two low-line, stone-topped tables interlock to form a versatile eating platform and display space.
3. Extroverted, sculptural furniture in look-at-me pink brings a sense of theatre to a pared-back interior.
4. A slim console table helps delineate zones in an open-plan living area and diverts attention from the plain back of the sofa.

1. A pair of ottomans gives greater flexibility to a formal arrangement by standing in for a second sofa, doubling as coffee tables or serving as footstools. The custom-made pieces replicate the style of the armchairs.

2. The fireplace provides a natural focus for an intimate sitting area between dining and family living zones. Warm reds and chocolate browns create a club-like feeling, while the blond-wood coffee table carries through a theme from the surrounding decor.

3. A blackberry coloured wall provides an intimate setting for a cherrywood dining table and chairs. The tapered legs give a lightness to the solid timber design, while cushioned seats provide the required comfort for leisurely entertaining.

4. Woven wicker and natural hues, lifted with splashes of red and sky blue, evoke the relaxed comfort of a provincial farmhouse. A large wicker hamper stands in for a coffee table, while the wrought iron and woven seagrass chair makes a pleasing ensemble with its matching footstool-cum-side table. The seagrass rug anchors the grouping.

5. Furniture that backs onto a glazed wall needs to stand up to scrutiny when viewed from outside – a criteria fulfilled by these classic 1930s armchairs. The strong horizontal line of the blackwood cabinet plays down the lofty height of the ceiling.

5

ARRANGEMENT

Furniture plays a very important role in defining the different activity zones of open-plan areas and creating logical flows for traffic. For instance, the straight back of a long sofa forms an obvious boundary between sitting and dining areas, as well as indicating the line of movement through a space.

Screens are useful devices for sectioning off areas or hiding an ugly view. Rugs similarly mark out the zones, drawing together separate groupings of furniture.

How you arrange your furniture is a matter of juggling scale and proportion and creating balance within the space. To save the strain of moving furniture to experiment with different groupings, make a to-scale floor plan of the room on graph paper, marking doors, windows, fireplaces and other fixtures, then use pre-cut shapes or sketch out various combinations.

As a rule, square rooms allow for easy groupings of furniture. You'll find that a long, narrow room works best when the seating is grouped to divide the space into two square areas.

GROUND RULES

● Where several doors open onto a room, pull furniture away from the walls into a central zone with clear traffic paths around it.

● To make a room appear larger, keep the corners bare and free from clutter, or opt for built-ins.

● Create congenial places to gather by arranging seating around a focal point, such as a fireplace or window.

● The television is often the focus, but not every seat should be angled to force its occupant to face the box.

● In a big room, choose furniture to match the scale. Think over-sized sofas in just-off-the floor designs. Even a small room will appear more spacious by including over-sized pieces with smaller ones.

● Balance the visual highs and lows by hanging artworks at the same height as tall cabinets and armoires or, where furniture is floor-hugging, positioning paintings at eye level.

● Reserve lavish fabrics for a one-off chair, ottomans and cushions.

● Loose covers are great for protecting or disguising upholstery.

livingfurniture

HOME ENTERTAINMENT

Entertainment isn't all about boxes with remote controls. It can be as low-tech as reading a book or having a chat. Your priority equipment in a living room shouldn't be a television; it should be comfortable seating and somewhere to rest a cup of coffee. Yet technology still has its place.

Usually the debate is whether to hide the television or not. But keeping video gear in a cupboard isn't just for neat freaks; it also puts it out of reach of toddlers. If your 'TV in a cupboard' is on a pivot, you can pull it forward for easy viewing.

Entertainment units, with their shelves and glass doors, are just one practical option. Place the television at seated eye level, stack the hi-fi above it and the video and/or DVD and games console below so children can access them easily.

With digital broadcasting, televisions are becoming bigger. Most used to be in a 4:3 ratio (4 wide: 3 high), but digital broadcast is best viewed on a wide-screen format with a 16:9 ratio (16 wide: 9 high).

If you are worried about a big television dominating the space, arrange the seating so the screen is not the focus of attention. Also take heart from the fact that 'thin is in'. New plasma screens are so slim they can be hung on the wall.

SOUND GEAR

Conventional stereos already have two speakers as part of the system, but home theatre systems need at least five to deliver surround sound. Satellite speakers are much smaller and less intrusive, but they need a sub-woofer (usually a largish cube) in the set-up to satisfy bass addicts.

What you have on the floor will affect acoustics. Sound bounces off hard floors but is deadened by carpets. Timber floors reflect sound more cleanly and are often the best choice for rooms with hi-fis.

Audio equipment also means audio cables. If you're renovating, you can conceal them away in bulkheads, but for most people it's a case of running them along the walls, out of the way of foot traffic.

1. With their sleek lines, the hi-fi and television in this apartment are made to be shown off. The wall-hung CD player is designed as a piece of art. A custom-built audio display unit gives the equipment a home, while cabling to other speakers is hidden in the bulkheads. The arrangement of sofas and ottomans keeps conversation, rather than the television screen, as the room's focus.
2. When this television is not in use, it is hidden away behind closed cupboard doors, visually streamlining the room.
3. The television and video are at the centre of this custom-designed storage unit in European beech veneer, but are hidden behind cupboard doors (which open, then slide back) when not in use. Full-size speakers are on glide-out tracks and CDs are stored in drawers.

3

living arrangement&detail

In the same way that a beautiful pair of shoes and bag can complete an outfit, so do decorative accessories complete the look of a room. As the final addition to a decorating scheme, they are the one thing that personalises a space, identifying it as yours. Accessories and accent pieces make it feasible to create new looks without any major drama. However, great rooms aren't made in an instant. A room's sense of place grows with time. Because rooms evolve as we do, they must respond to a family's changing demands. Some things insist on being displayed alone, and others need friends. The main thing to remember is to create an original arrangement in which no object disappoints or fails to please the eye.

1. Equally important in decoration is the sense of balance and the overall feeling of a room. But what makes it really interesting is mixing the unexpected, a bit of humour with quite serious pieces as well as flippancy with solidity. Wine goblets become an artform sprouting greenery in a perfect row. They are a foil to the tactile pomanders that tumble randomly from their woven wicker bowl, cleverly matched to the coffee table. A touch of whimsy comes from the painted canvas which was matched in scale to the cabinet.

2. First impressions count. In this entrance hall, where the indoors meets the outdoors, refined country accents reflecting the house's interior style are set in composition with potted greenery and unglazed terracotta.

1

2

3

4

5

6

7

8

9

1. Careful planning can make the difference as to whether displays appear dynamically creative or dreadfully cluttered. Here, symmetry is maintained and it works because there are few items to tire the eye.

2. If you enjoy having found objects around you, make a place for them on a tabletop. Quizzical and humorous items can be related either by colour, shape or texture. Here, a small assortment of disparate pieces echo the earthy neutral colour theme of the room.

3. A simple white candle has far more impact when it has comrades. The soft glow is reinforced and the effect is much more stylish. On a classic marble mantel set against dark moody walls, it brings a modern touch.

4. Items displayed on a table must be of a similar scale to the furniture, so avoid placing very large objects on small tables. Group candles so that there is a rise and fall in shapes and sizes and combine varying colours for interest.

5. It's easy to be intimidated by an expanse of blank wall, however partial you are to a pared-back, minimalist look. Some walls, however, are too short for an elaborate display. Instead, capitalise on this space to show off something different, like this French drummer boy's uniform. Neatly preserved in a Perspex box, the uniform adds colour and drama while giving importance to a collection of cocktail requisites positioned beneath.

6. In an open-plan living space, everything is on show, so be mindful of how objects are presented. For instance, a pile of fresh green apples will look more appealing in a white china bowl than in an old plastic container on the benchtop.

7. Don't overlook the inexpensive. If an object appeals, but loses merit on its own, make a group. The art of arrangement may be something as simple as a bowl of fruit placed on a bare wooden tabletop to echo the colour of a fabric or painting.

8. Savour the beauty of simple things that already surround you and the joy to be had in adapting objects at hand to new uses. Here, wicker baskets and gardening equipment sit prettily on open shelves while waiting to be put to use.

9. For the most impact, gather several figurines or statues together in a single display. In this instance, visual attraction results from strength in numbers. You can highlight the patina of the objects by positioning them in front of a dark background.

10. If you want to theme your prints, place them in frames of the same colour and style. In small, intimate spaces, framed prints and paintings are better composed in a square rather than hung single file along a wall. Colour accents should be positioned so that there is balanced harmony, for instance in cushions. And it's the little things that count; cushions look more professional when trimmed with fringing.

1. If arranged with an eye to balance and scale, even quite disparate objects can make a beautiful display. Don't restrict the idea to one room, either. Arrange a display in a place where all the family can enjoy it, whether they're eating a meal or simply walking through the space.

2. In a room that relies heavily on its outlook to the water for inspiration, a single bowl in vibrant orange is enough to create an impact. The colour is picked up in a vase of freshly picked zinnias placed strategically on the other side of the wood heater.

3. It's the details that define. Where a kitchen opens to a family living space, the *batterie de cuisine* adds a touch of shimmer and shine which can be picked up in other accessories further afield. These polished copper pots and pans are heirlooms.

4. A small, narrow space challenges creativity and initiative. Here, a mirrored wall and mirror-topped decorative plinth play with reflections. Wall art and objects have been scaled to suit the space, with the eye drawn to the velvety maroon wall. Chrome drawer pulls add polished accents.

5. One dramatic piece of art has the power to pull a room together. It also offers the catalyst for a colour scheme. In this long, narrow renovated kitchen/living space, a painting echoes those colours found on the kitchen benchtop and on the big easy chairs, making the vital connection between the spaces.

6. Possessions have a way of becoming a part of your life, and they can certainly enrich a home. On the other hand, clutter is the enemy of a great home. Invest some thought into how your possessions will be displayed. Once you do, you transform 'a jumble of things' into an eye-catching collection.

3 **4**

5 **6**

kitchen

The modern family kitchen has more bench space and storage areas than in the past, and is divided into zones to suit the individual family's lifestyle.

A few generations ago no-one paid much attention to the design of the kitchen. It was deliberately located away from life in the rest of the house and kept the cook out of the mainstream. How times have changed. The gradual shift of a woman's place from boss of the kitchen to a key player in the work force has liberated the kitchen from drudgery and given it new focus. At last the kitchen has come out of hiding and into the spotlight; it's the heart and soul of the home where we are nourished both physically and emotionally. It's no longer a basic utility area but a smart, stylish contemporary space zoned to meet the needs of family life.

kitchenzones

The kitchen is a room you spend a lot of time in and an awful lot of money renovating. Frankly, if the kitchen functions well, then life is on track. If it's difficult to work in, you'll start and end your day stressed. Today's open-plan kitchen is where you entertain friends, supervise the children's homework and basically run the house as 'the family business'. Cooking and eating habits have changed and the design of the kitchen reflects this. With today's emphasis on casual living, there is no longer such a need for a formal dining room. To make the best use of your kitchen space, first identify all the activities that will take place there, both cooking and non-cooking, and then allocate the zones accordingly.

1. FOOD PREPARATION

This is the centre of the action in a kitchen. Try to gear the design of this area to the type of food being prepared: fresh and fast warrants long, wide benchtops with easy access to the fridge and freezer. If you have a big family, then the bench should be able to take eight dinner plates laid out. Worth considering, too, is how many cooks there will be in the kitchen. Plan the under-bench storage so it can take knives, chopping boards and utensils. Food storage should be only a step away.

2. COOKING

This zone depends entirely on your preferred cooking style. Today there's more emphasis on grilling food, wok and stove-top cooking, and the consequent multi-burners and indoor barbecues have expanded the cooking zone. Singles and the time-poor can get by with only a cooktop and microwave, but if you cater for more than five or like to entertain, then give space to at least one oven or a heavy-duty range. Allow one metre of bench on the right-hand side of the cooktop (the reverse for left-handed cooks) as landing space for pots and pans.

3. EATING AREA

Open-plan blurs the boundaries between food preparation and eating areas, so you may want to give back a degree of privacy to the dining area. Consider locating the table away from the mainstream of kitchen activity or partially screening it from the view of people moving through the open space. Locate a cupboard for storing glasses, china and so on near the dining table. Of course, before you buy your dining table, measure it to make sure it actually fits in the room.

4. CLEANING UP

Washing up becomes easier if you choose a sink and dishwasher on the strength of the amount of actual cleaning up you have to do. Even with a dishwasher, you'll still need a deep sink for washing pots and large platters. To move and work comfortably, allocate up to one metre of space on the active side of the sink and above the dishwasher. If you install a smaller rinsing sink as well, this will extend the space further. The sink area itself demands under-bench storage for cleaning gear, perhaps a bin for food scraps and a container for recycling cans and glass.

5. ENTERTAINING ZONE

Today the question of where to entertain is answered quite simply… in the kitchen. Bound up as it is with an increasingly popular informal style of eating, the kitchen can be dressed up or down depending on the party. If you enjoy giving cocktail parties, assign the breakfast bar another job. If you have large family gatherings, make the focus of your entertaining the dining table and extend the mood to other areas of the living space. For television viewing, restrict the size and position of the set so it doesn't intrude when guests are around. And if you're the consummate entertainer, allocate storage for wine, a drinks cabinet, and a spot for CDs, DVDs and videos.

6. STORAGE

Appropriate storage should be planned around the activity zones of sink, cooktop and fridge. Plan for a mix of shelves, drawers and cupboards. Storage requirements essentially depend on whether you're into eating in or eating out. If you cook with plenty of fresh produce, you may not need a large pantry, but you will need storage areas away from the hot and steamy cooktop. For the busy family or the convenience cook, a well laid out pantry is imperative. Functional storage is all about organisation and access; when starting from scratch, sit down and make a list that includes absolutely everything you'll want to store in your kitchen.

7. BREAKFAST

Breakfasting in the kitchen is more than a lifestyle choice; often it's the only place to find a chair to sit down. Plan the location of the table early on when designing your kitchen. Consider the best source of natural light and make sure the spot is out of the traffic route. If you have children, include a breakfast bar in the L-shaped or open-plan layout of your kitchen. A peninsula bench under which stools can be tucked is just as good. But if morning rush hour means breakfast on the run, just allocate a parking space at the end of a work bench.

8. COOLING

Cold food storage is a linchpin of the modern kitchen. Before you buy a refrigerator and/or freezer, look at whether your cooking is focused on fresh foods or convenience foods; how often you freeze meals; and whether you shop daily, weekly or monthly. No matter how big or small your fridge/freezer is, make sure it's only a step or two from the food preparation area and can be easily accessed. And if you want one of the bigger combined fridge/freezers, remember to allocate enough floor space. Under-bench fridges or ones integrated into the cabinets are less flexible, but more discreet.

9. COMMUNICATION

This zone usually evolves by accident rather than design. The kitchen is the centre of the home, and it's where you tend to chat and leave messages for other household members, so it's worth considering the advantages of a dedicated communication station here. Set out of the main traffic route, it's where you can make phone calls in peace and recharge mobiles, receive faxes, use the computer to e-shop, and find your keys, shopping lists and school notes in a hurry. A corner spot or a small table is ideal, but remember to factor in the position of power points and cables, and storage for disks and stationery.

kitchen**layout**

The floor plan is the starting point for any new kitchen. The layout you choose depends on the basic size and shape of the space – there is no one ideal layout, except the one that suits you and your family. With the kitchen's reformed status as the new-age living room, it is tempting to forget that it's primarily the cook's workplace. A carefully planned layout that connects sink, cooktop and food storage areas is what you need. The shorter the distance between each, the more efficient the kitchen. It's best to plot your layout from the sink as it's the most expensive item to move because of plumbing. And although there are standard cupboard heights and bench widths, there's also a great sense of freedom in kitchen design.

GROUND RULES
- Bending below the bench is more tiring than stretching above.
- Do not place drawers in corners because it's too difficult to pull them open.
- Consider which way a cupboard door will swing when plotting your design.
- Don't set cupboard doors flush to the wall, as you won't be able to fully open the door. Instead, have a 'filler' section so door hinges are at least 2.5cm from the wall.
- Have at least one metre on each side of the sink and between the sink and cooktop.
- Install the dishwasher next to the sink for easy loading.
- Don't put a bank of drawers next to the cooktop. Children might use them as steps.

ORDER OF DESIGN
1. Position the sink and dishwasher.
2. Place the cooktop within easy reach of the sink and decide where to put the oven.
3. Plan the food preparation area within reach of the cooktop.
4. Keep the fridge away from main traffic and the stove, but near the preparation area.
5. Position the breakfast table or bar near natural light but away from cooking zones.
6. Plan storage so it's easily accessible from the kitchen's main activity zone.

1. GALLEY
Devised to maximise space, this style has two facing rows of benches set 1.2 metres apart to allow cupboard doors to open.
Advantages Perfect for small-space living.
Disadvantages Limited space for large appliances.

2. CORRIDOR
This is a single-file layout, with the cooktop, sink, dishwasher and under-bench fridge along one wall.
Advantages Good for small spaces and it can be screened with sliding or panelled doors.
Disadvantages No room for anything other than necessities.

3. ISLAND

The island bench locks the cook into a tight but efficient work pattern and demarcates cooking and living zones.

Advantages It suits an open-plan design where the kitchen is adjacent to a living space. The cook isn't shut away and can interact with guests or supervise kids' homework from the kitchen. If you're a messy cook, choose a bench with a raised back to screen the clutter.

Disadvantages The cost of relocating the dishwasher and cooktop into the island bench could be a deterrent.

4. L-SHAPED

This kitchen layout wraps around the perimeter and integrates with the living room. It is referred to as a peninsula floor plan when the L projects into the centre of the room.

Advantages It's the perfect layout for a combined living/dining room and provides potential space for a breakfast bar. The open floor space allows for a dining table while not interfering with the traffic route.

Disadvantages Cupboard corners often end up neglected and you'll probably need a lazy susan to make the most of under-bench space.

5. U-SHAPED

The U-shaped layout goes around three sides of a room with a window as a focus. It is safe and efficient.

Advantages Size is not a problem, which means the layout works as well for an apartment as it does for a big family home.

Disadvantages This layout can alienate the cook somewhat as most of the meal preparation is done facing a wall. The corners of built-in cupboards are potentially 'dead' areas for storage, so you may want to add some freestanding units.

6. OPEN-PLAN

Not all the work benches are uniform in an open-plan layout, as the kitchen has to cope with the home's busy cross traffic. The work triangle is confined to one corner, where the cook can keep an eye on children at play outdoors.

Advantages It allows many options for storage of key items.

Disadvantages In a smaller space, it could be difficult to avoid placing the fridge next to the cooktop. The actual amount of functional benchtop is small, even though the kitchen appears to be spacious and airy.

kitchenstyle

The style of your kitchen can reveal as much about your personality as the car you drive. So before you put pen to paper and begin to consider floor plans and cooktops, it's vital to discover exactly what style of person you are. Take an honest look at how you and your family live. If you detest clutter, you'll be happy with a minimalist style of kitchen with banks of discreet storage. If you like to chat, you'll enjoy an open-plan design. Remember, kitchens are no longer bound by four walls. The common feature of today's liberated kitchen is the originality that comes from blending different shapes and styles. Elements are mixed and matched with ease, drawing inspiration from the farthest reaches of the globe.

1. RESTAURANT

Fashionable restaurants with an open kitchen exposing the chef at work over a steamy cooktop have inspired the latest trend for at-home dining. The restaurant-style kitchen has the preparation area, dishwasher and sinks lined up to maximise the floor area. The cooktop is installed in an island bench with a serving counter that doubles as a family snack bar. Highly contrasting finishes such as dark woods, white walls and polished metal give this look its signature. Commercial-grade stainless steel typifies this style, creating an ultra-practical finish for benchtops and kickboard.

2. ECLECTIC

It's not so much about what goes into the kitchen as how it's put together. Eclectic style is interpreted by the young and the young-at-heart as a place to display a disparate range of elements. At its core is the modern freestanding stove and an unconventional mix of storage units. This style results in an unfitted appearance, without the streamlined integration of kitchen surfaces and appliances. Eclectic style isn't meant to be a cop-out where you can dump second-hand furniture with second-class appliances. In the confident, purposeful hands of someone with a sense of humour and a keen eye for design, the eclectic kitchen is the most original style of all.

3. INTEGRATED

Incorporating the kitchen into the living room is a sensible solution when space is at a premium. It's a common renovating choice for those wishing to update an older-style cottage or terrace house. Joinery and storage are designed to complement living room furniture and may make use of the same fine timber. If the room opens to a deck, terrace or paved outdoor area, then the flooring can be a device to link indoors with out. Food preparation and cooking areas should be sufficiently compact to avoid projecting into the main thoroughfare. It's a look that has small-family suitability while also being perfect for the professional couple who prefer to entertain at ease.

4. CANTEEN

The immediacy of food prepared and cooked in full view and brought directly to the table is part of the Asian eating-out experience. There, everyone sits at a long narrow table in the centre of the room. Many restaurants have adopted this canteen style of eating with the focus on one big waist-height timber table at which you perch on bar stools to eat your sushi and noodles. This style also suits a large, active family on the move. In such a household there's always a requirement for an easily maintained, multi-purpose work surface.

4

kitchenstyle

5. RETRO
This look displays the more understated, refined side of retro, with the emphasis on a sophisticated combination of colours like chartreuse and mustard, and materials such as mahogany and teak. Furniture with an industrial edge, timber laminates and the linear shapes of mid 20th-century design translate into a slick city look. Stainless steel becomes the accent, while marble, terrazzo, glass mosaics and exotic timber veneers create originality.

6. MINIMALIST
It takes a certain amount of conviction and discipline to carry off the minimalist look in a kitchen. It's a style associated more with the urban than the suburban. The look is all about space, light and an absence of superfluous detail – something which seems at odds with the kitchen and its many obvious components. The secret is to make tradition work in a contemporary way: storage must be discreet and fixtures, fittings and appliances intelligently streamlined. It's a provocative style based on dramatic design principles.

7. MODERN VICTORIAN
This style offers the perfect solution for those wishing to marry modern conveniences with traditional architecture. The scrubbed-clean, utilitarian approach of stark white-painted walls and wood, and tiles laid in a brickwork pattern is today offset by vibrant accessories and designer furniture. Time-honoured, hardworking linoleum features for the flooring, yet it looks fresh and modern in a bright colour and pattern. Drawer handles and panelled doors echo the style of old-time kitchens. Low-maintenance, functional surfaces and finishes retain this look's original spirit.

8. FARMHOUSE

This kitchen style has become almost as popular in the suburbs as it once was in the country homestead. The key to this look is its attention to detail and quality craftsmanship. Recycled materials add to the warm, lived-in appeal. A central work bench or classic butcher's block is the focus of the room. Limed, panelled or moulded cupboard doors, open shelves and wicker storage baskets, a laboratory sink and tapware, hand-painted tiles and a metal carriage with a *batterie de cuisine* are captivating elements.

9. DINER

Dispensing with conventional design and highlighting a lively mix of shiny chrome, etched mirror and pastel laminates, the diner was the social hub of many a small town, and a favourite location for film-makers. Today's funky re-creation introduces a contemporary approach, with the old metal-edged laminate breakfast counter and vinyl-covered swivel stools replaced by metallic-look polyurethane finished cabinets, brushed stainless-steel fittings, an Australian hardwood benchtop and designer-look bar stools.

10. TRADITIONAL

This is probably the ideal family kitchen because there's no guessing where anything is; the surfaces are low-maintenance and kid-proof, and the cook can be seen and heard but has a reasonable degree of privacy from the other areas of the home. The style is reinforced by the classic door hardware, marble slab benches, porcelain sink and glass-fronted cupboards with traditional push-back catches. It's an especially useful style for all those collectors who would like a safe place to show off their precious china or silver.

kitchen colour

The world was not made in black and white. Of all the rooms in the house, the modern kitchen is a testament to this. Colour is literally built into the kitchen with its cabinets, benchtops and splashbacks, so it's important to get it right. Replacing too-bright cupboards is a much costlier job than repainting a wall. Rather than making a fashion statement, choose colours that complement your lifestyle. As the kitchen has expanded into the family living area and outdoors, its decorative potential has increased dramatically, paving the way for a more expansive use of colour in finishes, appliances and accessories.

1. MONOCHROMATIC
White-on-white emphasises the three-dimensional quality of space by using variations of the one tone to add overall depth. A polished concrete bench and brushed stainless-steel appliances are 'shadowed' against the stark white walls and laminate cupboards of this kitchen, giving a fresh, modern, no-fuss feel.

2. RELATED COLOURS
The combination of colours which sit close to or next to each other on the colour wheel (see page 24) is what gives this kitchen its intrinsic warmth and personality. Cabinetry is in rock maple and jarrah, both warm-toned woods, and a feature wall and structural column are painted in claret red, which encourages appetite as well as energy. The darker colours appear to advance, adding drama to the space.

3. COMPLEMENTARY WITH TERTIARY COLOURS
The balance of warm and cool colours, those that are opposites on the tertiary colour wheel (see page 24), gives a kitchen clout. Designed for easy family living, this space uses geometric blocks of colour to 'streamline' the layout: warm aubergine for cabinetry with walls in contrasting cool 'dirty' green.

4. NEUTRALS WITH WARM ACCENTS
In a 'textured' kitchen with a great many finishes, the neutral 'tone' of the room is broken by a warm highlight colour. Here, burnt orange not only encourages the appetite, but also inspires confidence and stimulates the mind. It is used minimally but boldly in this room, seen in the occasional furniture and Aboriginal artwork.

5. NEUTRALS WITH COOL ACCENTS

The key to the success of this scheme is to use the cool accent colour with conviction. The deep blue in the mosaics and paint has impact but isn't overwhelming. The neutral colour of the pear-wood laminate cupboards and benchtops tempers the cool bite of blue and white.

6. COMPLEMENTARY WITH PRIMARY AND SECONDARY COLOURS

This kitchen's spirited look is based around contrasting colours of equal intensity (see colour wheel on page 24). Cool teal green and fiery red are underscored by the neutral combination of honey-hued Canadian maple and soft grey stainless steel. This is a balanced scheme, ideal for modern apartments and active family living.

9

1. A bowl of fresh rambutans brings a contrast of colour to a simple white noodle bowl.
2. Kitchen surfaces bring their own colour. Stainless-steel appliances and utensils add soft grey and silver to the mix.
3. Decorative glass in punchy colours clamours for attention. Glossy black tiles work as the perfect foil for the vivid glass.
4. For a shot of vibrancy, tuck a tiny tropical orchid into each napkin ring or in a little glass.
5. Using old, treasured pieces in new ways is the focus of this modern setting, where heirloom cutlery contrasts with a raw concrete tabletop.
6. Today's food is all about individual style; add a burst of brilliant colour to the table with tiny individual serves of chilled gazpacho.
7. A stack of Italian handmade pasta or salad plates adds festive colour to any home.
8. There's a carnival of colour to be had from the local vegetable market, so make some bright-skinned purchases the centrepiece of your table.
9. Pure and fresh, white works anywhere, particularly against warm wood. A collection of olive oils and herb vinegars add their own colour and texture.

ACCESSORISING

If you don't have the raw confidence to go it alone, paintbrush in hand, wielding expansive planes of bold colour, the intelligent solution is to add smaller splashes of colour to your kitchen and dining space with accessories (see left). Less is more when it comes to choosing accessories, and the same rule applies to the amount of colour you add to the space.

With today's unstructured style of eating, overdressed tables and fussed-over flowers all belong to a decade past. So, too, do cupboards crammed with patterned china and knick-knacks decorating the walls. In modern mode, crockery and dinnerware, decorative serving platters, cutlery, glasses and napery are mixed and matched with eclectic flair. Today, accessorising is all about putting together the things you really like.

COLOUR RULES
● Colour is built into a kitchen, in the cabinets and splashbacks. Get it right as mistakes are costly to fix.
● Put together a design board. Collect paint colour samples, tiles, laminate and so on. Lay them out on a piece of card to judge whether they work together.
● Decide where in the kitchen you want to emphasise colour; will you use it as an accent on white, or have bold sweeps of colour?
● Let the kitchen surfaces create the scheme. Stainless steel introduces silver grey, and timber can be any colour from cream to ebony.
● Cupboard doors, benchtops or feature walls can supply the colour against a muted background.
● Link a kitchen with the living area by using variations of the main colour.

kitchenstorage

Good storage is the key to an efficient, easy to use kitchen. It's even more important when the kitchen has assumed a web of roles, from dining room to laundry, each with its attendant clutter. And these days, time-poor families shop less frequently but buy more, so need more room to store groceries. Add to this the proliferation of kitchen gadgets, and it's plain to see why you need planned storage.

GENERAL STORAGE

● Avoid long, repetitive runs by mixing under-bench and floor-to-ceiling units as well as open and closed storage.

● Hiding major appliances behind cupboard panels will create a cohesive look.

● Cupboards over work surfaces should be shallow enough to allow headroom and make their contents accessible. But go easy on overhead storage if you don't want a small space to feel oppressive.

● Units on castors can be stored under a workbench and pulled out to provide an additional tabletop when required.

● Turn dead space into storage. A carousel or lazy susan makes a corner junction of cupboards into a viable storage space, and a slim vertical slot can house chopping boards or a pull-out pantry unit.

● Cupboards can be made to work harder with a range of fittings (racks, baskets, hooks, pull-out shelves) available from specialist storage shops.

● Open shelves are versatile and easy on the wallet. Consider the size and weight of the objects to be stored before deciding on the shelves' thickness and span.

● Drawers are easier to keep organised than cupboards and can be customised

for specific needs, such as tiered sections for cutlery or a lift-out receptacle for compost scraps. It's also easier to retrieve a pan from a deep drawer than from the back of a cupboard.

● Opt for tried-and-tested devices such as a ceiling-mounted rack with butchers' hooks to hang pots and pans or a wall-mounted rack for a *batterie de cuisine*. A timber butcher's block with built-in knife storage and drawers is also useful.

● Baskets provide dark, well-ventilated storage for dry goods, bread, root vegetables or table linen.

● Racks under the cooktop are great for storing and drying off pans, providing that dust and grease are kept in check.

FOOD STORAGE

● Where space permits, include a walk-in pantry. It needs to be cool, dark and well ventilated, and have plenty of shelves, becoming shallower with increasing height to make access easier. Allocate space for appliances and include power points so you can use them in the pantry.

● Consider the type of food that you'll be storing. This will determine whether you will need lots of freezer space, racks for storing tins, bottles and jars, and places for stowing fresh fruit and vegetables.

● A new development is fridge and freezer drawers, which are put at strategic points around the kitchen. These have variable temperature and humidity controls to keep food at optimum freshness.

● If you're storing wine, make sure wine racks are away from the stove and fridge.

● A slim-line, pull-out unit placed next to the cooktop is ideal for storing oils, sauces and seasonings for cooking.

FINISHES

Increasingly, kitchen storage is looking like furniture, with refined finishes and hardware. Where the kitchen forms part of the living area, it must be at ease with the overall design of the space. But choose a finish that can cope with the workload, or chic will quickly become shabby.

Laminate Inexpensive and easy to clean, laminate comes in a huge range of colours and patterns. It is prone to scratching (except for high-pressure laminates) and may lift at the edges if continually wet.

Timber It has a natural warmth and solid integrity, but is expensive, environmentally costly (especially if from non-sustainable sources) and may warp if not properly kiln-dried or acclimatised. Softwoods, such as pine, can dent easily.

Veneers These give the appearance of solid wood at less cost and with less impact on the environment. They can be shaped far more easily than solid wood but may lift in damp conditions.

Stainless steel An attractive, durable finish that's best combined with other materials to prevent it looking too clinical. It won't chip, rust or tarnish, but will scratch and needs frequent polishing to remove finger marks and splashes.

Glass It creates an airy, open feel, but for safety reasons you'll need toughened glass, which is more expensive. It shows finger marks but is easy to clean.

Painted Paint offers infinite decorative possibilities, from traditional matt finishes to spray-painted lacquered effects. Choose enamels to cope with grease and moisture. Paint isn't as durable as some other finishes, but surfaces may be repaired by repainting.

2

3

4

5

6

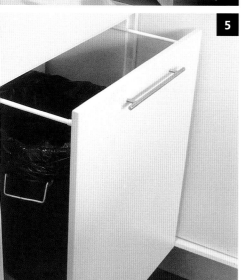

1. Storage at its most simple: a bowl of colourful nectarines ripe for the picking.

2. Kitchen-style storage is modified to meet the needs of the adjacent dining space, with display shelves and a built-in console providing storage for tableware. Finishes are consistent to ensure visual continuity.

3. A series of low-set alcoves storing large serving plates, platters and bowls provides visual relief in a long run of sleek white units.

4. A clever, compact kitchen fit-out presents a polished face to the adjoining living space, with food preparation hidden behind the high-backed island bench. Spices are kept handy to the stove in two vertical racks, and the microwave is integrated into the overhead units to free up bench space. The breakfast bar doubles as a servery to the deck beyond.

5. Dedicated storage for the garbage bin in a pull-out drawer keeps it accessible yet discreetly hidden.

6. Salvaged restaurant fittings, like this stainless-steel drawer once used to collect coffee grounds and now housing cooking utensils, bring industrial strength and style to the contemporary kitchen.

1

2

3

4

5

6

7

8

9

1. A walk-through pantry lined with floor-to-ceiling cupboards and display shelves takes the storage pressure off the kitchen. A tiny office space slots into the far end, serviced with shelves, drawers and a telephone.

2. Deep kitchen drawers are practical for stowing saucepans, crockery and other heavy items at an easily accessed height.

3. An appliance port is a great timesaver, with equipment plugged in and ready for action. Appliances can be quickly stored out of sight to leave the worktop free of clutter.

4. Under-bench cupboards are fitted with slide-out shelves to ensure that crockery and glassware is safely stored and within easy reach.

5. This arrangement of kitchen units balances concealed and display storage. A white panel screens the kitchen bench from the adjoining living space.

6. Here, storage is designed as an architectural element and finished in colourful laminates. The sense of fun extends to the offset sink unit.

7. A pull-out pantry allows easy access to all items and banishes the dead zone which often lurks at the back of kitchen cupboards. Racks can be raised or lowered according to need.

8. Providing storage and display space, this massive French shop-fitter's cabinet is also a design element in a predominantly white kitchen.

9. This heavy wooden bench, salvaged from an aircraft factory, was the starting point for an unfitted kitchen improvised from recycled elements. Pull-out wicker baskets provide dark, ventilated storage for dry goods.

10. This island bench has dedicated spaces for baking trays, pots and pans, and a top shelf to stack tableware. Cutlery and utensils are stored in the drawers.

10

PLANNING CHECKLIST

● Get rid of anything that you haven't used in the past six months.

● Get a clear idea of what you need to accommodate, measuring individual items if necessary, and not forgetting about space for cookbooks and non-food-related things such as mops, the vacuum cleaner and ironing board. Divide your cookware, crockery, glassware, utensils, table linen and appliances into separate groups on the floor to gauge the area each requires, allowing extra for future additions.

● Try to strike a balance between open shelves and closed cupboards for a better visual effect.

● Items used on a daily basis should be stowed on the worktop or stored between hip and eye level to save you bending and stretching. Rarely used items should be stored in the dead zone above 2 metres from floor level.

● Store kitchen items close to where you will use them: utensils and pans near the cooktop, mugs near the kettle, cutlery and crockery close to the dishwasher and table, recycling bins close to the sink, compost collection bin next to the food preparation area, and appliances next to a power point. Similarly, plan specific storage to serve the different zones within the kitchen: a cupboard for household paperwork or children's craft materials near the kitchen table and stationery storage for a home office space.

● Be realistic and make storage relevant to you and the way you live: there's no point having plenty of display space, for instance, if you're not prepared to keep it dust-free and organised.

● Standard off-the-shelf units are cheaper than custom-designed pieces. If you want a more unusual timber or laminate, consider buying stock carcasses and custom-designing the doors rather than building from scratch. Bear in mind that flat-fronted doors are less costly than shaped or panelled designs.

walls&floors

People cooking, even eating, can be tough on walls and floors. It's these surfaces that must withstand the spills and splatters of daily life, and it's disastrous if they're not up to the job. Specify the right surfaces for the life your kitchen leads. Here, being easy to wipe down is just as important as looking good.

1

WALLS

The walls in a cooking zone have to be tough. Food splashes and steam are all part of the scene here.

Paint must be washable. Go for a semi-sheen rather than an ultra matt finish, so cleaning won't leave any telltale shiny marks. If you're using wallpaper above your cooking zone, choose a vinyl one – moisture gets under normal wallpaper, making it mouldy and causing it to peel.

The wall behind the cooktop is usually protected by a splashback of tiles, glass or metal. Extending the splashback material to the ceiling gives a designer effect with the bonus of protecting more of the wall.

You can also put a section of wall to practical use by fitting a panel of cork or plywood painted with blackboard paint to use for shopping lists or messages.

PRACTICAL FLOORING

Floors in kitchen/dining areas must be durable, washable and non-slip. Vinyl, linoleum, cork, rubber, wood and hard flooring are all practical choices here.

You may want to use different flooring in your dining area, or have the same material in both for a unified look. If you use different flooring, make sure the transition is smooth. Joins should be neat with no change in the level of the floor.

Whatever floor you choose, you'll be living with it for a long time. You'll find that polished wood or flooring in a neutral shade adapts most easily to different decorating styles and is less likely to date.

HARD FLOORS

Hard floors are the most durable in the kitchen/living nexus, but they're murder on dropped glasses. You can soften the landing by laying mats in potential drop zones near the sink and dining table.

Glazed tiles are a favourite in cooking areas as they're unaffected by heat, water or oil and are easy to clean. Choose a style with a non-slip surface for safety.

Remember, too, that although the tiles themselves may be stainproof, the grouting between them can stain, so use grout suitably coloured for camouflage.

Unglazed terracotta and quarry tiles give a room a warm, earthy base, but must be sealed or they'll soak up oil and dirt.

Stone, concrete and traditional terrazzo, which uses cement as a binder, also need sealing, otherwise they will absorb stains. However terrazzo made with resin in place of the cement does not stain as readily. Remember, too, you need a honed rather than a polished surface for safety.

TIMBER FLOORS

Timber is a natural for an open-plan kitchen/living space. It looks good, is hard-wearing and resists most food stains if it's properly sealed. But avoid having too much 'groove' in your tongue-and-groove floor, as the gap will trap food scraps, and clean up any spills as they happen. And don't stomp across it in your stiletto heels – you'll leave dents. Be wary of parquet in the kitchen, too, as it may lift if saturated.

If your budget doesn't extend to wood, cheat with a laminate floating floor. Made of plastic-coated wood or cork veneer moulded to a plywood base, the tongue-and-groove sections can be laid over an existing floor and are virtually stainproof.

RESILIENT FLOORS

Resilient flooring is quieter to live with and kinder on legs and dropped plates than other floors. Hard-wearing linoleum was a favourite up to the 1950s, and is undergoing a revival. However it's vinyl that now rules in the kitchen. Waterproof, oil-proof and easy care, it's no surprise vinyl has become so popular.

Cork and rubber are also good in the kitchen, but cork should be well sealed to resist spills. For rubber, choose a textured pattern (rubber is slippery when wet) and avoid unpolished matt rubber – it marks easily and soaks up oil spills.

1. A Peperino stone floor unites this kitchen and dining area. Stone is immensely hard-wearing, but expensive and heavy. Make sure the sub-floor can take the weight. **2.** Although not as durable as tongue-and-groove timber floors, stained and varnished marine plywood can take the heat in the kitchen and comes at an affordable price. **3.** The sweep of this kitchen/dining area is emphasised by the polished timber boards. A floor-to-ceiling glass 'wall' gives an uninterrupted view of the pool outside. The timber veneer wall at right houses the kitchen pantry.

1. Large floor tiles are laid on the diagonal so things look less 'square'. It's a clever way of visually pushing out the walls to make a space seem bigger.
2. Linoleum's eco-friendly credentials and serviceability have seen it come back into fashion, but a custom-designed pattern like this is in the luxury price range.
3. Timber is a versatile material. Here a herringbone parquetry floor contrasts with the light European quilted birch veneer used on the cupboards.
4. Visual textures combine in this scheme. Cupboards and walls feature particle board, sanded and clear finished. The flooring is the original timber boards and the ceiling is ripple iron. Even the painted finish on the feature wall echoes the pattern of the particle board.

HARD FLOORS
TILES
Tiles must be laid over a flat, rigid base – concrete screed is best. If you have a timber floor, lay hardboard on top first, otherwise the movement of the floorboards will eventually crack the tile adhesive and the tiles will lift. Also check that the floor is strong enough to take the weight of the tiles. Unglazed terracotta and quarry tiles need to be sealed or they'll soak up oil and dirt like a sponge. Ask a tile specialist for advice.

STONE
A stone floor works brilliantly in areas that extend from indoors to out, but it comes at a budget-busting price and is very heavy. Check whether your sub-floor is strong enough to hold the stone first. Stone slabs, which can be 80mm or more thick, must be laid in a cement bed over a concrete sub-floor. Stone tiles are thinner, about 10mm, less expensive, and much less heavy. For safety, use stone with a non-slip, honed finish rather than a polished finish. Granite is the toughest, most dense stone and also the priciest. Slate is waterproof. Limestone comes in an incredible range of colours, but is porous so should be sealed to prevent staining. Sandstone, too, needs sealing. Ask your stone supplier for advice.

TERRAZZO
Terrazzo is an aggregate of marble or granite chips mixed with concrete, which can be trowelled or rolled onto a concrete or a screed base. It's laid in 8-metre panels, divided by brass or zinc strips, then ground to a smooth finish. It's so strong, the terrazzo can be as thin as 9mm. It's also available as tiles, which are laid as usual.

CONCRETE
Concrete makes an affordable heat- and scratch-resistant floor, but it can look a bit brutal if left in its 'natural' state. Mixing coloured oxides into the cement before it's poured makes it more glamorous. When it's cured, seal its surface with several coats of acrylic or epoxy resin so it doesn't soak up spills. For a softer look, apply several coats of commercial paste wax and give it a machine buff. Or simply paint with paving paint. Concrete can be poured over existing tiled floors.

RESILIENT FLOORS
LINOLEUM
Linoleum is made of linseed oil, ground cork, wood, flour and resin which is baked and pressed onto a jute or hessian backing. It comes either as tiles or sheeting, and should be laid on a flat timber or fibreboard floor.

VINYL
Sold as tiles or sheets, vinyl is waterproof, oil-proof and easy care. Vinyl contains PVC (polyvinyl chloride), which gives it its flexibility. The more PVC, the better the product. Cushioned vinyl, with an interlayer of foam, and vinyl backed with foam rubber are the most resilient. It wears best when laid over a flat floor, but can be laid straight over existing flooring. The downside is that vinyl doesn't wear its age well, is easily marked by scrapes and rubber (which leaves black stains), and the product itself is non-biodegradable.

CORK
A 1970s favourite, cork tiles are soft and warm underfoot. The thicker the tile, the more resilient the floor. Cork tiles must be laid on a flat surface; you may need to cover floorboards with plywood or hardboard. Don't lay cork tiles over underfloor heating or directly on concrete (lay a damp-proof membrane beneath) or they will lift. After laying, seal the cork with four coats of polyurethane or polymer sealant to protect it against dirt and moisture.

RUBBER
Mostly sold as tiles, rubber flooring is quiet, warm and hard-wearing. But smooth rubber can get slippery when wet – you might be better off with a studded pattern. Unpolished matt rubber marks easily and sucks up oil spills, so in busy areas protect it with a polish of water-soluble wax emulsion. Repeat the polish from time to time.

kitchenlighting&windows

The kitchen and eating area is the nerve centre of many households, and the lighting has to be up to scratch for the space to function properly. Preparation areas in the kitchen need to be well lit so you can see what you're doing, but that same intensity of light in a dining area will create a cold, clinical feel. What you need is a combination of ambient and task lighting, and that takes a little planning.

NATURAL LIGHT

A kitchen/eating space that glows with sunlight always looks welcoming. It gives you a gentle wake-up buzz at breakfast and will lift spirits throughout the day. But you should ensure that an expanse of glass doesn't mean too much heat. The cooktop and oven already warm up the room, and untamed sunshine could make the temperature unbearable.

Windows on the sunny side of your home should be shaded with blinds or shutters (curtains aren't a good idea in a kitchen as they absorb odours) and sky-lights should be shaded or have an opaque finish to minimise heat transfer.

1. Glass doors and windows, framed in anodised aluminium, pull in the sunshine to this city apartment. The polished hardwood floor, stainless-steel benchtops and white ceilings and walls bounce the light for maximum effect. Adjustable spotlights are fitted throughout the apartment, and can be focused where needed at night.
2. Twin windows over the sink allow in natural light at work-bench level, while those above the cabinets diffuse sunlight across the ceiling. A row of pendant lights focus on the wide bench, which is used by its owner for cooking classes.

3. Loads of natural light and fresh air make this kitchen warm and welcoming. French doors connect the indoors and out and a trio of opening skylights lets the sunshine play across the ceiling. The skylights have a double layer of glass with venetian blinds between – a practical combination that minimises heat transfer and glare. The sunlight reflects off the stainless-steel benchtop and marble-topped breakfast bar below. Low-voltage downlights illuminate the space at night.

5

6

1. The light fantastic takes centre stage in this dramatic design, which combines task lighting and ventilation in the one unit. The white ceiling and benchtop reflect the bulbs' glow, while twin downlights in the exhaust fan structure get close to the action.

2. This vaulted space includes a kitchen and dining/living area. The adjacent deck, accessed through sliding doors, adds to the living space. High louvres and clerestory windows allow in light and air, so the room glows without sunbaking.

3. Extending the dining zone onto a deck is a sensible move in a subtropical climate, and this galley-style kitchen is part of a spacious upstairs living area. Two sets of bi-fold doors and an unusual strutted window work as a 'wall' which can be folded away to unite inside and out.

4. Sunshine falls through glass doors and a deep window, set high in the void over the eating area in this townhouse. A Murano glass pendant light brings grace to the dining table. In the kitchen, low-voltage halogen downlights illuminate the marble benchtop.

5. Three slim hopper windows add to the tailored good looks of this kitchen. A benchtop of pale limestone bounces sunshine into the room, and low-voltage halogen lights on a wire track take over at night.

6. Pale walls, Italian sandstone flooring, terrazzo benchtops and stainless-steel mosaics on the splashback move the natural light around this kitchen/living room. Roller blinds can be pulled down to keep the sun in check. Downlights are fitted in a bulkhead over the kitchen.

SURFACES AND LIGHT

Surfaces either reflect or absorb light and this has a big effect on the overall level of illumination in a room. A white surface reflects 80 per cent of the light that hits it and gloss and shiny surfaces, such as stainless steel, also bounce light.

A kitchen with stainless-steel appliances and glazed tiles can give one light source a lot of movement, effectively shifting the beam right around the room. A pale or polished timber floor can even reflect light from the ceiling to help illuminate under-bench cupboards.

On the other hand, darker colours and matt surfaces, such as brick or plaster walls and unglazed tile floors, absorb the light. So if your kitchen has a dark colour scheme or a lot of matt finishes, you'll need to include more sources of light to compensate for this effect.

1

A PRACTICAL LIGHTING PLAN
- Target directional lights on the cooktop, oven and preparation areas, or fit strip lighting beneath overhead cupboards to work as task lighting.
- Have an overhead light, with a dimmer, in the eating area.
- Locate sinks and preparation areas close to windows for natural light.
- Have enough ambient light so you can see easily into cupboards.
- Keep fluorescents to the kitchen, where their light creates less shadow. The pink or green cast of fluorescent light makes food look unappetising, so tungsten or halogen bulbs are better in eating zones.

VENTILATION

Windows don't only let in light – just as importantly, they allow in air. Although most recently renovated kitchens include a rangehood to take steam and cooking smells outside, when it comes to keeping a kitchen and adjoining living area fresh, nothing beats natural cross-ventilation.

Remember, small windows placed at ceiling height are just as good for moving cool air through a space as standard windows, and they also avoid the problem of a cross-breeze turning into a gale.

And don't ignore the view through a window or glazed doors – it can be as important a part of a room as the decor.

1. Glazed walls around the dining area mean this room basks in sunshine. The cooking zone benefits from the clerestory windows pulling in light from above, but is out of the direct sun to avoid problems with heat. Small, ceiling-height windows allow good cross-ventilation.
2. This kitchen/dining/living area works as an informal indoor-outdoor room. A custom-built 1200 x 1800mm skylight lets in as much light as possible to the room's centre, while red-cedar bi-fold doors open the area to the deck.

kitchenbenchtops&splashbacks

The humble kitchen bench and splashback see a lot of living, and their colour and pattern sets the kitchen's design theme in one fell swoop. Benchtops must be functional and good-looking, and with splashbacks now stretching from cooktop to rangehood, being easy to clean has become a top priority.

LAMINATE

The most popular benchtop material can also be formed into a splashback, and is available in thousands of colours.

Advantages It's economical, waterproof (if edges are sealed properly), easy to clean and heat-resistant. Post-formed laminates allow curved, seamless fronts.

Disadvantages Knife cuts cause irreparable damage; it does deteriorate over time.

Cost Low to medium.

TILE

Ceramic tiles offer endless possibilities in colour and pattern for benchtops and splashbacks. Choose from either glazed or fully vitrified tiles for benchtops. They are usually set into cement or stuck straight onto a baseboard and grouted in. Standard tiles or ceramic or glass mosaics can be selected for splashbacks. In certain situations, the mosaic splashback is extended beyond the cooktop area to the ceiling, creating a dramatic focal point.

Advantages Hard-wearing, waterproof, heat- and stain-resistant, tiles are also reasonably easy to keep clean. Available in a huge range of colours and styles.

Disadvantages Tiles are hard but could crack or chip if subjected to excessive weight and wear. It's the grouting that will let you down, so choose a stainproof grout in a colour to blend with the tile.

Cost Low to medium.

TIMBER

Hardwood benchtops made from solid plank, glue-laminated or recycled woods are attractive and very popular.

Advantages Wood adds warmth and colour and suits most kitchen styles.

Disadvantages Must be finished with a polyurethane sealer, water-repellent oil or varnish. Knife cuts and direct heat will damage the surface, but it can be repaired.

Cost Medium.

STAINLESS STEEL

The choice of chefs everywhere, stainless steel is a near-perfect benchtop material.

Advantages Strong, heatproof and low maintenance, it suits stainless-steel appliances and timber cabinetry.

Disadvantages It scratches easily and shows finger and water marks. Carbon-steel objects, like knives, can rust and mark its surface. It's costly to fabricate into curved shapes and noisy unless insulated.

Cost Medium to high.

CONCRETE

Concrete is a current favourite with those who love an industrial look. It's mixed with additives to make it less susceptible to chipping and is sealed and polished.

Advantages Concrete can be cast in any shape and has a robust, seamless surface.

Disadvantages Things dropped on it will break. It must be expertly sealed or it will stain. It can take several weeks for the concrete to cure after being poured.

Cost Medium to high.

MARBLE AND LIMESTONE

Marble has an old-world elegance, while limestone suits contemporary styles and comes in a range of colours.

Advantages Heatproof and there are many colours to choose from.

Disadvantages Marble is cold and hard, but not as durable as granite. Both marble and limestone are porous and will stain if not treated with a penetrating sealer.

Cost Medium to high.

GRANITE

The ultimate for durability, granite slabs come with square or bullnosed edges.

Advantages It is non-porous and impervious to food acid, heat and marks.

Disadvantages As granite is heavy, base cupboards may need to be reinforced. Knife blades will go blunt if you cut on this surface. Polished granite invites finger marks; hone it instead for subtle texture.

Cost High.

TERRAZZO

This is a thin composite of marble, granite, stone or glass chips set in a coloured cement slab and polished and sealed.

Advantages It is hard-wearing, waterproof and can be customised.

Disadvantages Items will break when dropped on it and it must be sealed every 12 months. Patterns can go out of style.

Cost High.

1. Both durable and fashionable, stainless steel is formed into the benchtops and splashback in this kitchen, with glass mosaic tiles providing contrast in colour and texture.
2. Twin polished stainless-steel sinks are recessed into a benchtop of Marina Verde granite. The mixer tap has a special rinsing head.
3. The work zones of this kitchen feature benchtops in laminated ash while the serving bench (just seen at left) is a polished limestone slab. The splashback is glass, a sleeker option than tiles and easier to clean.
4. A free-form polished concrete bench does double duty as a table for casual meals.

1

2

3

4

5

6

7

8

9

1. A dark wenge timber slab makes a chic island bench that doubles as a dining and sometime work space.
2. Bianco Sando granite and mirror create an airy mood.
3. A stainless-steel sink is teamed with tapware in a satin nickel finish and a splashback of glass mosaics.
4. Aubergine-coloured laminate benchtops make a rich contrast to beech veneer cupboards and a stainless-steel splashback.
5. Colour-backed glass and polished stainless steel form a lively duo in this kitchen.
6. Sinks are fabricated as part of a stainless-steel bench.
7. Benchtops in high-gloss white laminate and a splashback in bronzed mirror reflect light.
8. The raised marble 'privacy screen' on this island bench hides cooking clutter.
9. A porcelain Belfast-style sink is set into a recycled timber bench, reclaimed from a disused aircraft factory.

BENCH HEIGHTS

The standard height for a kitchen bench is 90cm, with a width of 60cm, but in an ideal kitchen, bench heights should be higher or lower to suit the activity. Try 5cm to 10cm below bent elbow height for food preparation; 5cm below the base of a bent elbow for the top of the sink; 17cm to 25cm below elbow height for a surface where appliances are used; one low bench for pastry-rolling (or children's homework), and a higher one for serving food such as in an island bench breakfast bar. Bear in mind at the planning stage that particularly tall or short people will need work surfaces adjusted to their own height.

SOLID SURFACES

These include synthetic solid colour resin materials and composites which combine resin with chips of stone, glass or mirror.
Advantages Extremely durable and hard-wearing. Surfaces are seamless and the colour goes all the way through. They can be formed to any design, including the sink and splashback, making them ideal for kitchens with awkward bench shapes.
Disadvantages Some surfaces look 'dense' and have no light-reflective qualities. They're difficult to install without professional help, which hikes up the price.
Cost Very high.

GLASS AND MIRROR

Toughened glass or mirror are brilliant splashback options because of their smoothness, which makes them super-easy to clean. Toughened glass can be clear, frosted or colour-backed (sprayed on one side with paint of your choice). They are available in sheet or tile.
Advantages Glass has a beautiful light-reflecting translucency and in sheet form it is very easy to keep clean. Reflections from a mirror splashback add light and movement to the kitchen.
Disadvantages Both will chip if heavily knocked. Mirror is high maintenance.
Cost Medium to high.

SINKS

The sink plays a major role in the kitchen, as the place to rinse vegetables or clean pots and pans. Tailor the sink (or sinks) to your needs. Is it to be used solely for pans and oven trays, or for hand-washing china and glasses, too?

Generally speaking, big and simple are best. Compact single-bowl sinks designed for smaller kitchens are fine if you're a microwave cook and do minimal food preparation. But it's worth investing in twin basins or one large bowl and one small bowl if you have a family or entertain regularly, as it will simplify washing, rinsing and food preparation.

As far as shape goes, think deep and square. Oval and round sink bowls make cleaning platters, baking trays, woks and heavy cast-iron pans very difficult indeed.

A boxy Belfast sink (see photo 9) is a traditional design that works very well. It is wide, deep and robust, and because it is fitted without a frame, there is only a short distance to reach over into the sink.

SINK MATERIALS

Stainless steel is the most common material used for sinks. It comes in different gauges, and the thicker the gauge, the quieter, sturdier and pricier the sink. Other metal options are copper and brass.

Although generally more expensive than stainless steel, porcelain is enjoying a revival in popularity and presents a stain- and heat-resistant surface. Styles in porcelain include the traditional Belfast and laboratory-inspired sinks.

A sink can also be moulded from a synthetic solid surface material. The customised installation makes it expensive, but the result is seamless and sleek.

TAPS

The best taps turn on at a touch. Choose from single-lever taps, mixer taps which integrate hot and cold water, separate pillar taps which keep temperatures separate, laboratory-style taps with levers you can turn on with your elbows if your hands are messy, and pull-out mixer sprays for rinsing vegetables.

To avoid the dreaded drips, choose taps fitted with ceramic discs. Don't waste time with any other kind.

Look for taps with a hard, smooth finish. Chrome-coated brass taps stay shiny for years. Nickel-plated taps cost more; heavy-duty plastic taps cost less.

kitchenappliances

As the kitchen has been integrated into the dining/living area, kitchen appliances have become fashion accessories. Now that they're out on show, appliances are looking funky as well as being functional. The way we cook has also changed. During the week, dinner must be fast – sometimes it's a quick reheat in the microwave or something cooked up in a wok or on a grill. It could even be a cafe-style snack, made for one person rather than a family. Weekends are another story. Cooking is for relaxation and everyone joins in. The indoor-outdoor way of life has also seen the humble barbecue grow into an outdoor kitchen. With its own side burners and a roasting hood, it's as useful as the kitchen for turning out meals.

OVENS

Most ovens are electric as they give a more even heat than gas models. In a gas oven, there's only one heat source and it tends to be hotter at the top than the bottom.

Most electric ovens have two elements: one for baking and roasting, and another at the top for grilling. Some ovens switch on the top element during baking to give more even browning.

Fan-forced, convection ovens use a fan to circulate the heated air for faster, more even cooking. This is a timesaver, but can dry out some foods, and the fan can also be quite noisy when it's on.

Self-cleaning ovens are a boon for overworked cooks. Pyrolitic ovens superheat up to 500 degrees Celsius, turning baked-on debris to powder which is then easily wiped off. Steam-cleaned ovens heat a mixture of water and detergent to 60 degrees Celsius to soften grease.

Practicalities Standard size ovens are 60cm wide, but larger 70cm and 90cm models are available for cooks who like to entertain. Ovens are safest when fitted into the wall at eye-height, so you don't have to bend over steaming, hot food. Sometimes it can be difficult to reach into a high-set, front-opening oven, so maybe a model with a side-opening door would suit you better. Of course, if space is squeezy, you can always put the oven below the bench, under the cooktop. Have 40cm of bench space near the oven where you can place the hot food.

MICROWAVE OVENS

The ultimate timesavers, microwave ovens cook by 'exciting' molecules through the food. But as the air inside stays at room temperature, the food won't crisp. Combination microwave ovens get around this by including conventional heating elements: you can cook in microwave or conventional mode or combine the two.

Practicalities Have a 40cm landing space below or adjacent to the microwave oven. To avoid accidents, set it at a height that young children can't reach – adult eye-height is a good level.

COOKTOPS

There are several sorts of cooktops, including up-market combination cooktops where you mix and match electric or gas burners, wok burners, deep-fryers, barbecue grills and steamers.

Gas burners These provide instant heat and are preferred by chefs. Gas is good at delivering the high heat required for stir-frying, but it can be a little tricky keeping the flame going for a very low heat.

Electric cooktops Electric is the better option for long, slow cooking. Even electric-coil elements, the cheapest option in electric cooktops, retain heat. Solid disc elements, made of cast iron, are slower to heat and cool but easier to clean.

Ceramic-glass cooktops have electric coils or halogen elements fitted beneath the glass. Halogen units heat faster than the electric coils, but cost more to run.

Smooth magnetic-induction cooktops do not get hot. Instead, an electro-magnetic element generates heat directly in the base of the pan to cook the food. But it only works if the pan is flat-bottomed and made of a ferrous metal, such as iron or stainless steel. Aluminium and copper pans will stay cold. Test a pan's base with a magnet – if the magnet sticks, the pan will heat with magnetic induction.

Practicalities For safe, easy cooking, allow 60cm of space above a cooktop and 45cm on each side. Have control knobs at the front, rather than the side, to avoid passing your hand over steaming pans.

1. A pull-up board solves plug-in problems on an island bench.
2. Now the kitchen's part of the open-plan living space, appliances are dressing up. A stainless-steel cooktop, oven and rangehood are the centrepiece in this kitchen. The colour of the stainless-steel benchtops continues with the polished concrete island bench.
3. More stainless steel, this time on a built-in espresso machine slotted between sleek ovens.
4. This super-smooth ceramic-glass cooktop has control knobs at the front of the cabinet, well away from steam and splatters. Mirrored overhead cupboards, with strip lighting beneath, maximise light in this slim work space.

1

2

3

VENTILATION

Open-plan kitchen/dining/living spaces need good ventilation if you're to keep the smell of curry out of the couch. And it's not just cooking odours that linger; steam from bubbling pots and dishwashers must be dispelled as well. Having good cross-ventilation in the room is a big help, but you'll still need to remove steam and fumes at the source by fitting an exhaust system.

Ducted rangehoods These are an up-draught system that pulls air through a filter and outside through a duct.

Down-draught systems These can either be flush with the cooktop or sit up to 15cm above it at the back. They swallow fumes into ducting which runs under the floor and outside.

Recirculating extractor fans These filter out some odours and steam through charcoal pads, then recirculate the air into the room. They're less effective than ducted systems, but cheaper to install.

1. Floor-to-ceiling concertina doors help fully integrate the kitchen and outdoor space in this city home. The stainless-steel kitchen bench extends beyond the doors onto the deck, and is fitted with a gas barbecue and extra gas burners for the ultimate in outdoor cooking. There is even a basin.
2. This combination cooktop has two ceramic-glass electric hotplates (at left), two gas burners and a larger wok burner.
3. Freestanding stoves are still popular in the kitchen. While they lack the versatility of a separate cooktop and oven, they're cheaper and easier to install.

Practicalities A rangehood should extend over the entire cooktop and be from 60 to 75cm above it. If you have a barbecue grill, you'll need a rangehood with more power to cope with the smoke. Good rangehoods or extractors shift from 450 cubic metres of air an hour, but there are models that move 950 cubic metres an hour. Twin filters are more effective than single filters, and those with a fine, close-knit mesh will trap more grease.

FRIDGES/FREEZERS

As life gets busier, fridges have become bigger. Rather than buying food daily, you're more likely to shop every two weeks, so the fridge and freezer must be able to store a trolley-full of food. Separate temperature controls on meat and vegetable compartments allow your food to be kept in the best environment for each.

Where once there was no choice other than white in fridges, there is now a range of colours or, if you prefer, stainless steel. Many fridges can have a panel fitted to the front to integrate them with the kitchen cabinets.

Side-by-side models have narrower double doors – a good thing when clearance is a little tight – but come in larger, family-friendly sizes. The top-of-the-range models include automatic ice makers and in-door ice and filtered water dispensers.

The fridge eats up the most power in the kitchen, so buy the most efficient model you can. The more stars on the energy-rating sticker, the more energy efficient the fridge is. For the same capacity, top-freezer models are slightly more efficient than those with bottom freezers.

Practicalities Leave a small gap between the back of the fridge and the wall for ventilation. Keep a 40cm landing space on the handle side of your fridge, or within one metre. It makes taking things out of the fridge easier, so the door is open for less time and loses less cold air.

DISHWASHERS

A dishwasher releases you from sink-side drudgery. It also washes dishes at higher temperatures than the human hand can stand, so is more hygienic, and deals with a full day's worth of dishes in the one go, using less water than if you had filled the sink three times that day.

To work best, dishwashers should be connected to cold water so they can heat the water to the optimum temperature for a wash cycle: around 40 degrees Celsius for glasses; 55 degrees Celsius for a normal wash; and 70 or 75 degrees Celsius for a pot cycle. A delayed start function lets you take advantage of cheaper electricity rates at night.

Dishwashers with separate drawers mean you can choose different cycles for each drawer or, if you have a small load, run just one to save on water and power.

Many dishwashers come with an option of fixing a panel to the front, so the machine is disguised as cabinetry.

Practicalities Standard dishwashers are 60cm wide and hold 12 to 14 place settings. Slimline models are 45cm wide, the same width as a standard kitchen cupboard, and can fit eight or nine place settings. Allow at least 60cm of bench space near the dishwasher to stack the clean items as you unload the machine.

SMALL APPLIANCES

As cafe food has become more popular, there's been an explosion in benchtop appliances. Cappuccino machines, breadmakers and flat grills for toasted sandwiches let you re-create that caffe latte taste at home, but they take up bench space. Tame the collection by storing it in a specific appliance cupboard, along with the electric jug, toaster and food processor. If possible, include adequate bench space and enough power points for the items to be used in situ, rather than taking up other preparation areas.

kitchenfurniture

The modern kitchen demands a range of furniture to service its many roles and define its character. Furniture demarcates zones within an open-plan space: an island bench can divide cooking and eating areas while a sofa with a high, straight back can set the limits of the living space and an alcove may serve as the home office, equipped with a stool, storage, telephone and other technology. The flexible, portable, stackable and stowable all have a place here, as furniture is moved around according to need.

1. These metal dining chairs, a 1950s design by Harry Bertoia, create a clean-lined cafe feel.
2. Furniture clearly establishes the zones in this one large multi-functional space. Casual eating at the breakfast bar gives way to more formal dining at the table setting beyond, and TV dinners on the lap in the sitting area at the far end. Kitchen cupboards are finished in hoop-pine veneer to imitate the living-room furniture.

THE TABLE

With the demise of the formal dining room, the kitchen increasingly serves as entertaining space as well as everyday diner, and the table is a key ingredient. Traditionally the table took its place in the centre of the kitchen, but today it may be in an adjacent space. Wherever you put your table, decide on the position early on in your planning.

As the room's natural focus, the table must be large enough to cope with several activities (food preparation, entertaining, homework, doing finances, hobbies and so on). Choose a table that can take the knocks and is easy to clean.

CHAIRS

The trend for stacking bistro and folding cafe-style chairs mirrors a more relaxed way of eating. Gone are the days of the perfectly matched dining suite; today it's more about mixing styles.

The chairs around a kitchen table should be comfortable and child-proof. Wipe-down, practical designs win out over upholstered chairs, which are prone to absorb kitchen smells and will get badly soiled if they're not protected with removable covers. Where chairs serve more than one space (dining area, kitchen and courtyard, for instance) choose light-weight, portable designs.

THE BAR

Built as an extension of the work bench or island unit, the breakfast bar supplements the family table and sometimes replaces it altogether. Where the bar wraps around a cooking zone, it should sit above the cooktop to screen untidy surfaces.

The best bar stools incorporate foot-rests and back supports. Make sure the stools and benchtop are of compatible heights, giving a minimum knee clearance of 30cm and allowing the elbows to rest comfortably on the counter.

Where possible, the breakfast bar should face the kitchen action or a window rather than a blank wall.

1 **2**

TABLE MANNERS

● A round table promotes more sociable gatherings. Traffic flows easily around them, especially in a square-shaped kitchen. In a small space or awkward corner, they seat more than the equivalent square or rectangular design. A table measuring one metre in diameter should comfortably seat four.
● An oval table is ideal for seating six. For flexibility, choose an extendable round table that converts to an oval.
● When it comes to seating large numbers, rectangular tables are more practical. Bench seating allows a square or rectangular table to fit snugly against a wall, and will seat more than an equivalent span of chairs.
● An extendable gateleg or wall-mounted fold-down table gives flexibility in a tight space, especially when teamed with folding chairs.
● Tables with central pedestals or slim legs accommodate more chairs.
● A table with built-in drawers can store tableware or children's playthings.

DINING AREAS

A separate dining room seems less of a luxury when it has additional functions, such as a home office. In this case, substitute hard-wearing materials for the highly polished furniture traditionally associated with this room. A sideboard or built-in cupboards can provide safe-keeping for dinnerware and stationery.

Many homes have an outdoor living space that extends off the kitchen. If you enjoy eating alfresco, it's worth investing in a well-made, outdoor dining setting.

When choosing furnishings, bear in mind that consistent colour keeps the look uncluttered, while mixing styles makes things more welcoming. For instance, a white laminate or stainless-steel kitchen will benefit from the warmth of an antique dresser. And including an unexpected item, such as a chandelier, helps play down the utilitarian function of the space.

1. Furniture in this open-plan kitchen/living area is casual and durable, with playful shapes and a bright palette. Robust red sofas, salvaged from a 1970s office fit-out, can take the knocks dished out by young children, and the kitchen table is a pine door fitted with legs.
2. This formal dining area is separated from the kitchen by a raised bench with a sliding glass panel. The custom-made table and Art Deco-inspired cocktail cabinet are consistent with the finishes used in the kitchen. Rich pommele sapele veneer and a waxed brushbox floor add to the formal appearance.
3. An orange Arne Jacobsen Egg chair forms a visual anchor in this open living space, and a set of white Verner Panton dining chairs provide strong, comfortable and stackable seating in the adjacent outdoor eating area.

kitchenlaundry

Laundries of old were steamy, down-at-heel places that were banished to the far reaches of the house. But with the advent of quieter washing machines and dryers, utility rooms have smartened up their act and found their way into the centre of the home. Increasingly, the laundry is housed in 'a cupboard' in the kitchen or bathroom, or off the living space, with smart cabinetry to match its surroundings.

1. This laundry has two washing machines, as well as a dryer, to allow light and dark loads to be washed simultaneously.
2. Deep drawers neatly stow gum boots and other gear.
3. Floor-to-ceiling cupboards hide appliances in this sleek laundry. The ironing station is a permanent fixture.
4. This functional laundry fits into a double kitchen cupboard.
5. Here, concertina doors disguise a laundry space off a dining area.
6. A slide-out ironing board is a great space-saver.

PLANNING

A dedicated laundry is still the ideal. As the obvious place to store general cleaning gear, it takes the pressure off the hard-working kitchen space. And where better to house the hot water service, meters, freezer and sewing machine, as well as do the ironing, craft projects or household maintenance jobs.

Where clothes are dried on a washing line, laundries should have direct access to the garden, to avoid a trek through the house with muddy boots and a basket of wet clothes. In households where the washing is dried in a dryer, utility rooms are increasingly located close to the bedrooms to ease the collection of dirty clothes. Similarly, laundry chutes save on legwork and make light work of teenage bedroom clutter.

Laundries generate lots of moisture, so ensure the space is well ventilated, preferably with plenty of natural light and airflow to minimise dampness and mildew.

Consider installing an extractor fan, use an anti-mould agent in the wall paint, and ensure the moist air from tumble-dryers is vented to the outdoors.

Only water-resistant, non-slip materials should be used in the fit-out, and flooring must slope to a wastehole for drainage. Check with your local authority for the minimum required distance between power points and water sources, and ensure lighting targets the work areas.

STACK AND STORE

A laundry that's at the rear of the house will be a natural dumping ground for shoes, coats, sports gear and school bags, and you'll need to provide appropriate storage for these items.

Kitchen-like built-in cupboards are the ideal, with tall cupboards or hooks for storing brooms and mops, pull-out racks for cleaning products, and a locked cabinet for harmful chemicals. A double sink is useful for hand-washing, soaking and

bleaching; fit it with a gooseneck tap with adequate clearance for filling a bucket.

Where space is limited, consider stacking the washer and dryer, or invest in a machine that combines the two roles. Include a table or benchtop for sorting clothes and a hanging rack to deal with rainy-day washing loads.

Minimise clutter with a pull-out or ceiling-mounted drying rail, a slide-out or flip-down ironing board, and a system of laundry baskets for different needs (white loads, dark loads, dry-cleaning, awaiting ironing and so on).

Where laundry services are housed in the kitchen, maintain the integrated look by placing the laundry appliances behind cupboard doors. As well as looking neater, this has the advantage of cutting out some of the noise and screening the whirling action of the washer or dryer – an important consideration when the surrounding area is also used as a place for eating and entertaining.

3 **4**

5 **6**

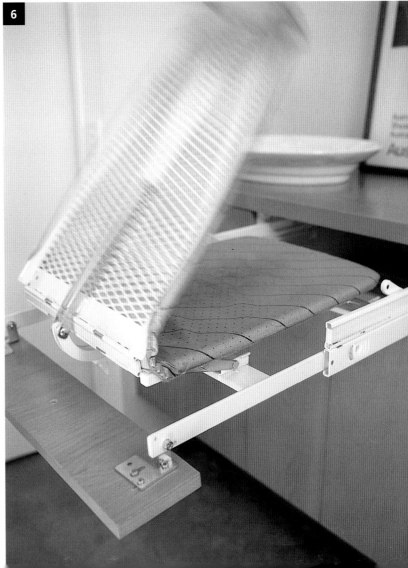

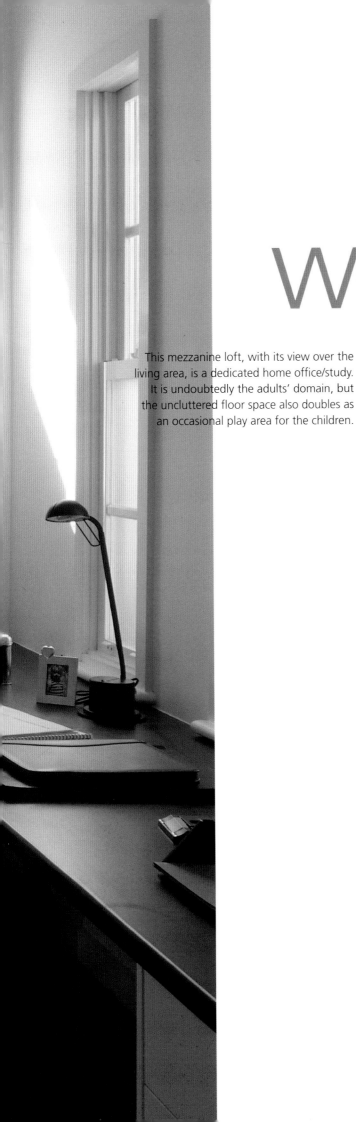

This mezzanine loft, with its view over the living area, is a dedicated home office/study. It is undoubtedly the adults' domain, but the uncluttered floor space also doubles as an occasional play area for the children.

working

Centuries ago it was common for retailers and traders to live above their shops. But during the Industrial Revolution, having a workplace separate from your home became the norm. Now work has come back to the nest. Without a doubt, the home office is here to stay, with an increasing number of people seeking to either nurture a career from home, undertake part-time studies or simply keep the household paperwork in check. You need to consider how distinct your work space should be. Whether it's a corner of the kitchen or living space, or a whole room set up as an office, you'll have to shape it to suit your family's lifestyle.

workingzones

When planning your home office, concentrate on making the space safe and comfortable and zone it to your specific work habits. Design the storage to the task, and make sure there is plenty of natural light and fresh air. Even if it's only for home accounts or surfing the internet, a well-ordered office is paramount.

1. ORIENTATION

If you're running a business from home, you will spend an inordinate amount of time at your desk. Give yourself every opportunity to take a break by providing easy access to the outdoors, natural light and plenty of fresh air. Not every home office has proximity to a swimming pool like this one, but having an escape to the outdoors can relieve tedium. In this case, the sliding door also means the office can be reached independently from the main house entrance.

2. MULTI-FUNCTION

Integrating an office into the heart of a busy household means setting aside an area strictly as a work station for computers and fax machine, and ensuring it can be screened off from family life. The dining table can do double duty as a 'boardroom' table and living-room shelving can be adjusted to take business files and disks. A second-storey addition is just what the home-office worker dreams of and this one suits the family's lifestyle to a tee.

3. & 4. PRIVACY

It's impossible to maintain a professional standard with an office space caught up in the melee of daily family life. Try to create a private zone so you can work in isolation at least some of the time. Designating a loft or mezzanine space as a home office makes sense because you can hear the family action below, but not be part of it. The journey becomes more important than the destination when family members have to make the trip up to see you, which, in effect, becomes a useful deterrent.

5. STORAGE

Split your work requisites into two: things you need to get at regularly, which should be as close to the desk as possible, and what you don't need on a daily basis, like reference materials. An area devoted to research books, magazines and files, such as a wall of open shelving or a bank of filing cabinets, can be away from the desk and phone. Sort out worktop clutter with small containers. Here, a 'library' wall connects this home office to a reading room.

2

3

4

5

workingstyle

Working from home is a brilliant way to escape the corporate world. But what's the point of abandoning the realm of suits if you then re-create that same stark stereotype at home? Get the ergonomics and the lighting right, then bring your personality to bear and turn the work space into your place.

1. HOME COMFORTS

There's no reason why the desk, seating and storage should look like they've migrated from the CBD. In a home office, the emphasis is on 'home'. Instead of laminate and metal, have desks and shelves made of timber. Hang artworks and lay a toe-tempting rug on the floor. Who's going to see if you're wearing shoes or not? This work studio is so self-sufficient it has its own kitchenette and bathroom. The home away from home mood is reinforced by a laze-on-me sofa and a beautiful work table that can serve for dining when needed. Narrow windows and opaque glass panels let in light without sacrificing privacy.

2. CASUAL

A more casual style can make working more appealing. Lighten the mood with a splash of brilliant colour, but don't sacrifice functionality for a funky look; always keep an eye on ergonomics. In this SOHO (small office home office), a laptop computer, extendable table and cordless phone put the focus on flexibility. Pristine white and orange accents proclaim a more relaxed approach.

3. OCCASIONAL

Your work space may simply be a place to sort out household bills, and a desk in a quiet corner may be all that's needed. In this situation, match furnishings to the rest of the room. A classic dining chair and French provincial writing table are not out of place in this guestroom-cum-study. Flooded with natural light, it's a welcoming spot to work.

4. INTEGRATED

A work space doesn't always command its own room. Often it's integrated into a guestroom, a bedroom (though this is best avoided), a dining or living area. Even if it shares a space, you'll want the work area to be fairly self-contained and quiet to avoid distractions. Remember, if you commandeer the dining table, you will have to tidy up every night. Choose a desk and chair that complement the room's scheme. A long desk and a modern dining chair make a super-smooth home office in this living area. Given its size, the desk is surprisingly unobtrusive, with its timber tones harmonising with the furnishings.

5. THE STUDY

Being able to close the door behind you gives a psychological break between work time and free time. The traditional study, with book-lined walls, paintings and hushed atmosphere, was in essence the original SOHO. Adapting the idea to a modern work space is easy. Remember, however, that a traditional roll-top desk is too shallow for most desktop computers and will lack convenient holes for power cords. This home office is an adult's retreat in a busy, child-filled house. The custom-built desk has small holes in the top to accommodate computer cords and the cupboards disguise a hanging filing system. The traditional decor is carried through from the nearby formal dining and living areas.

2

3

4

5

workingcolour

Colour affects the mood of the rooms you eat and sleep in, so why wouldn't it affect the space you work in? Typically, home offices have been places devoid of any real character, just depositories for the computer, fax, accounts and files. Yet mentally stimulating colours can improve motivation and enhance your creativity. Exercise your freedom and indulge yourself a little. Feel happy in your home's work space by choosing friendly colours that complement the light, both natural and artificial.

1. NEUTRALS WITH AN ACCENT COLOUR

Colour is intensified in a brilliant white room, which is why white is often the first choice of graphic artists, designers and painters for their at-home offices. But pure white is highly reflective and harsh on the eye, so temper it with accents of blues, purples and yellows. Here, a liberal dose of ultramarine blue creates the colour buzz in a superbly appointed home office.

2. COMPLEMENTARY COLOURS

Brown is a mix of red and violet dashed with black and is a warm colour. Green, however, is a secondary colour and cool (see colour wheel on page 24). These two colours create a complementary scheme. In this study/home office, they meet as accents in an essentially white room. If it were used over a larger area, the combination could be considered a little dull and uninspiring.

3. PRIMARY COLOURS

It's best to avoid classic fire-engine red, however a deeper, dustier shade of red, like brick, burgundy or even maroon, has the power to transform a small space into a warm, inviting and exciting working environment. Here, a once-grey attic comes alive in red tempered by the tones of wood and abundant natural daylight. Under artificial light, the space glows like a jewel.

3

4

5

COLOUR THERAPY FOR THE WORK SPACE

When deciding what colours will make you happy in your home office, consider:

- The amount of space and light you need.
- The comfort of the space.
- The air. Is there enough ventilation?
- The temperature. Is your workplace cold, hot, damp, etc?
- Your temperament. Can you sit for long periods? Are you hyperactive? Do you suffer insomnia or occasional depression?

Choosing the right colours can help you feel more comfortable in your own space. Try to achieve a balance of colour. For example, willow green and raspberry pink, which are complementary colours, could be chosen to offset sleeplessness and over-activity. Orange and yellow are mentally stimulating and are said to help those with a depressive nature.

4. & 5. USING ARTWORK

Striking, evocative images and motifs in the workplace are often overlooked, so make use of their colour to soften the industrial landscape. Here, a designer's creations provoke ideas for both colour and pattern (top); postcard scenes from Greece add vibrant blue and white (above).

workingstorage&equipment

The idea of a work space in the home is hardly new. Artists and craftspeople have traditionally devoted part of their living quarters to a studio or workshop, and grand houses have always had a formal study or library. The SOHO, or small home office, is the modern manifestation of such a space. Often, the decision to work from home is a lifestyle choice, reflecting a more relaxed approach to business and a desire to have greater flexibility. Yet whether it's a corner of the kitchen, a writing desk in a living room, or a dedicated office where clients are received, efficient storage is the key to a smooth running space.

1

2

3

4

1. The upper storey of a house provides a self-contained study space. Built-in bookshelves line the walkway between the reading room and the study area, four steps down. A long, deep writing desk is sized for serious study, with drawers for stationery and files.
2. This desk, purpose-built in Brazilian mahogany, conceals a hanging file system.
3. Horizontal plan cabinets, as used in architects' offices, are brilliant for stowing collections of photos and papers.
4. This custom-built cabinet has slots of different sizes to accommodate a range of paper. On the top is a casual collection of artworks.

DUAL-FUNCTION SPACE

Where space for a dedicated home office is lacking, the guestroom or dining room will often take on the load. Good storage is essential for juggling the roles, allowing worktops to be quickly cleared, and accessories and appliances to be screened or stowed out of sight. Storage and tables on castors lets you wheel away the work when the room returns to domestic mode.

Rather than using the dining table as a makeshift desk, it may be better to create a dedicated space where your work can be left undisturbed. A corner of the room or an alcove fitted with sliding or folding doors or a fabric blind will allow you to shut up shop at the end of the day.

Perhaps the ultimate in artful deceit is the office in a box, with finishes to match the decor of the host room. This can take the form of a specially designed cupboard or even an antique armoire customised to house a computer work station.

BUSINESS AND PLEASURE

A dedicated workroom can take its own cues when it comes to decor and storage. But when your SOHO is integrated into another room, it must be sympathetic to its surrounds. Grey metal filing cabinets will sit uncomfortably in most living spaces. Think outside the square and make use of fabric-covered boxes, lidded baskets or a customised antique desk rather than a utilitarian computer desk.

CIRCLE OF REACH

When planning your layout, allow one metre of clearance in front of a filing cabinet and 90cm in front of shelving. The worktop itself should be reserved for essentials such as the computer, lamp and phone. Dedicated computer desks, often fitted with castors, generally supply all your immediate storage needs, with integrated shelves, drawers, cupboards and alcoves for stowing everything from books and manuals to disks and pens.

Under-desk filing cabinets on castors can be pulled out to provide extra worktop space. Mobile units and small office trolleys fitted with suspension files or shelves are invaluable, especially when rooms have dual roles and you have to tidy up quickly. You can also use freestanding cabinets and shelving to zone off areas and create privacy around a desk.

SHELVING

You'll probably need to find additional space for books, magazines, files, back-up supplies of stationery and so on. Floor-to-ceiling cupboards, fitted with adjustable shelves, can absorb most if not all of these items, and hide away clutter.

If you opt for open bookshelves, break up a wall of tomes by including sections to display vases or pictures. Make use of the space above a window or door for a high shelf to store rarely used books or documents – and keep a stepladder handy.

It's easy to underestimate the weight of paper and books; shelving needs to be sturdy enough and have sufficient support brackets to take the strain.

TAMING CABLES

There should be enough power points for the computer and its peripherals, as well as the telephone, mobile phone charger, fax, kettle (for that welcome coffee), sound systems, heater, fan, lighting and all those other appliances that find their way into a home-office space.

Not only do these individual items need a home to keep the area neat, but all the cabling that comes as part of the package will require some sort of management system if it's not to become a chaotic tangle of leads.

Cabling ducts recessed into the walls or ceiling give the cleanest result, but an existing arrangement can be improved with devices that coil up the slack, bundle loose cables or run cable lengths in tracks fastened to the top of skirting boards.

workingsurfaces&lighting

There's no reason why a home office should look like a commercial office. You might as well make the most of home comforts, giving yourself a room with a view and abandoning workaday grey for something more sophisticated. Surfaces can be classy rather than corporate, but when it comes to lighting, follow the rules. Eyestrain is eyestrain, no matter where you are working.

1

1. This study has wool carpet underfoot to help keep things quiet. A trio of narrow windows above the desk and another fixed window to the side encourage the sunshine. For close-up work and reading, there is a halogen desk lamp.

2. A small bedroom becomes a functional office space when a custom-built desk is slotted into place. Art on the walls and a dense rug on the floor put the emphasis on comfort. An anglepoise desk lamp can be easily swivelled to direct light.

3. During the day, walls of glass make this stand-alone studio office feel part of the garden. At night, a trio of pendant lamps focuses light on the desk. Windows open to the south and west to catch breezes.

4. A comfortable chair and French provincial writing table turn this room with a view into an occasional office. The arched colonial-style window pulls in the sunshine, while at night a table lamp provides adequate task lighting.

WALLS AND FLOORS

There are no hard and fast rules about what's best on the walls and floors in a home office. If it's easy to live with, it will be easy to work with. Of course, if you're using paints and dyes for your work or hobby, you'll be happier with vinyl or tile on the floor than carpet.

With walls, remember that dark walls absorb light and make a room appear dim – a nasty formula for eyestrain.

Sound insulation is also important. If you need more hush in your work space, put carpet on the floor and choose upholstered chairs. You can also install sound insulating panels into the back of storage units or fit the panels to the walls and cover them with fabric. Floor-to-ceiling cork is another effective sound absorber and also makes a handy noticeboard.

LIGHTING

Task lighting is a home-office essential. You can install lights directly above your work area, but a desk lamp that swivels to focus light is the most effective option.

Ambient light should also be at a reasonable level; a high contrast between background and task lighting will tire eyes.

Hotspots of light, such as reflections off glossy surfaces or computer screens, also strain eyes. Position lights to avoid any hotspots and use a non-reflective desktop of wood rather than glass.

You should position the computer side-on to any windows so the sun doesn't shine directly onto the screen or straight into your eyes. If that's impossible, fit blinds or curtains to temper the glare.

AVOID OVERLOAD

Remember, one power point can take only 2400 watts before it overloads, even when there's a power board connected. Count the number of watts for each piece of equipment before plugging it in – you'll find it on the label on the back. A computer typically draws between 200 and 300 watts and a desk lamp uses 20 to 50 watts. A 2400-watt heater will trip that safety switch really fast!

workingfurniture

Adding personal touches, like a favourite painting, a leafy plant, comfortable sofa and decorative cushions, will make your home office or work space somewhere pleasurable to spend time. Select furniture that is stylish and contemporary, or combine the newer acquisitions with vintage pieces to create a space that nurtures originality and boosts self-esteem. Where space is tight, choose multi-functional, compact designs – you can create an area for work almost anywhere in your home.

HI-TECH TIPS

- Electronic equipment should be well ventilated and kept out of direct sunlight and other sources of heat.
- A dedicated power circuit with surge protection is good insurance for hi-tech equipment.
- A laptop computer makes fewer demands on space, but you're liable to get more neck strain than with a standard desktop computer.
- To economise on space, mount a computer on a bracket shelf to free up the desk, and have a pull-out keyboard shelf that slides under the worktop when not in use.
- A wall-mounted phone will also save on worktop space, especially in a corner of the kitchen devoted to household accounts and bill paying.

THE CHAIR

You should buy the best-quality chair you can. Dining or kitchen chairs are no stand-in for a desk chair. An ergonomic chair will provide the proper support for your back, neck and shoulders. It should be fully adjustable, forward and backward as well as up and down, and provide lower-back support. All this allows you to finetune your chair to the perfect seating position, which is to have your back upright, your elbows bent at 90 degrees, your body facing your computer screen, and your feet on the ground or on a footrest. For stability, choose a five-castor base over a four-castor design, and go for comfort with a well-cushioned seat covered in breathable upholstery fabric.

THE DESK/WORKSTATION

A desk that serves as a computer work station with plenty of integrated storage may be the best solution for a small space. But if your SOHO is in the dining room, you may well find the dining table also does duty as a desk. In a dual-function room, a desk with a raised side will help to enclose the designated work space.

The desktop should be 120-140cm wide by 75-85cm deep to fit a computer, and 68-73cm high. So you can manoeuvre your chair, leave a minimum of 85cm between your desk and the wall or piece of furniture behind it.

Try to make space for a comfy chair or sofa in your work space, too. It will provide a welcome chill-out zone.

1. The home office of a busy architect features a desk with a plan cabinet underneath, an ultra-comfortable Aeron designer swivel chair and shelving custom-made to fit folders and magazines.
2. For poring over plans and artworks, a low table and funky block-wood stool are ideal.
3. An interior designer's studio/home office has a custom-designed European beech veneer and steel desk and designer ergonomic chair.

bathroom

In the bathroom, it's not the quantity of space that's important, but how you use it. The bathroom has evolved from being a simple washroom to one with therapeutic value, a change which is in tune with the need to rekindle a sense of well-being. The ensuite, too, has gained new status. Once a poor cousin to the family bathroom, today it is quite often as spacious and frequently more resplendent. Even plunge pools and gym equipment have eased their way into the modern bathing space. Yet while the boundaries between other living spaces have blurred, the bathroom remains the one truly private retreat in the home — and somewhere you love to linger.

There is a real desire for today's bathroom to offer the luxury of a personal day spa. This bathroom is awash with sophisticated finishes and generous space. The twin square basins and a big double shower ease the pressure during morning peak hour.

bathroom**zones**

As today's lifestyles become ever more demanding, bathrooms are having to deliver new levels of comfort and relaxation. By night, these spaces are the ultimate chill-out zones, where you soak away the stresses of the day in deep baths or under massaging showers. But night-time calm soon gives way to morning madness and facilities can be stretched to capacity in the weekday rush to get out the door. Creating a space that can handle all this, as well as negotiating the plumbing, wiring and ventilation, often in tight confines, makes the bathroom one of the most challenging – and costly – rooms to design or renovate. One way to approach the problem is to define different activity zones.

1. BATH

Taking a bath is an everyday luxury. It allows you time out from the stresses of the day and is even more calming if you can enjoy a view of the garden while you bathe. Of course, if you have young children, their love of the 'bathtime ritual' is a major reason for having a bath in the first place. You can make it easier on your back by having a wide ledge next to the bath that doubles as a seat for you and a step into the tub for the little ones.

2. INTEGRATION

An ensuite is the ultimate personal space, shared only with your partner. Here, where there isn't space for two separate rooms, the bathing zone has been integrated into the bedroom itself. There should still be a delineation between washing and sleeping areas, as water and soft furnishings don't mix. It could be as simple as a change in flooring from carpet to tile, or a dividing screen.

3. RELAXING

The concept of relaxation has become important in bathrooms. Having a dimmer on the light switch means you can bathe in a gentle twilight. The addition of stereo speakers lets you enjoy music. Some bathrooms are large enough to accommodate a chair – perfect to perch on while painting your toes. In this light and airy boudoir, the bath itself marks the border between splash and sleep zones, contributing to the sense of space and serenity.

5

6

4. FITNESS

If your bathroom has the space, why not include an exercise bike? It gets the gear into a zone where there are already towels and a shower – just like a real gym. The fitness regimen doesn't have to stop there. Spa baths offer therapy for tired muscles, but weigh more than conventional baths, so make sure the floor can handle it.

5. MAKE-UP

A well laid out vanity area will soothe morning moods. As well as a basin, there should be enough storage for cosmetics and toiletries, power points for shavers and hair-dryers (at least 50cm from splash zones), an even light for putting on make-up and adequate bench space. Twin basins will ease traffic jams and a no-mist mirror can make life easier, too.

6. SHOWER

It's much faster to have an invigorating shower than take a bath and it uses less water (60 litres for a five-minute shower using a standard showerhead versus 80 litres for a bath). It's also much easier to fit a shower cubicle in a smallish room. Showerheads with a choice of sprays – pulsating, full flow or softly aerated – turn a shower into an indulgent experience. This generously sized cubicle has a showerhead on a sliding rail so it can be adjusted up or down. The mixer tap is located beyond the throw of the water, so there's less chance of an accidental scalding.

GROUND RULES

• Existing plumbing will often determine the position of the bath and other fixtures, especially the toilet.
• The first step should be to draw a plan of the room to scale, adding in cut-outs of basins, etc, and allowing enough space around them for easy access.
• Work out the position of towel rails or fitted shelves, plus power points. This is also the time to decide on underfloor heating, heated towel rails and exhaust fans.
• Where space is tight, opt for a roomy shower area instead of a bath, or economise on space by having a shower over the bath. You can also install a shorter bath across the width of the room rather than along its length.
• To get the comfort and facilities you really want, consider relocating the bathroom to a larger room in the house, or borrowing space from a neighbouring room.
• Setting a bath on a platform helps break up space and allows for storage shelves around its perimeter.
• If you have children, ease your mind by setting hot water in the bathroom to a maximum of 50°C. At 50°C, hot water takes five minutes to cause a major burn. However in most homes, the hot water is set to 65°C, which will scald a child in less than half a second.

bathroomstyle

Since the early days of cinema, interior designers and stylists have been hugely influenced by the on-screen bathroom. Once this room became more than a place for cleanliness and hygiene, it was imbued with images of luxury, glamour and opulence – not to mention sex. Today's modern family bathroom can comfortably mix the handmade with the man-made with elegant sophistication. Style should not take the place of function, however. Bathrooms have so little room for error, in terms of placement of fittings, that it is crucial you decide on the design style at the initial planning stage.

1. MODERN VICTORIAN

It was not until late in Queen Victoria's long reign that the bathroom was brought indoors. Most were distinguished by their large, decorated basins and big, footed roll-top baths. Many had chintzy wallpaper on the walls and freestanding furniture. A contemporary adaptation of this style does well in a Victorian terrace or Federation house renovated for today's family living. For a fresh take on an old theme, trade the paper for paint on the walls, remove the curtains and let in the sunlight.

2. MINIMALIST

To the minimalist, space and clean lines are more of a luxury than the most decadent fittings. Function becomes the only requirement in a room devoid of superfluous decoration. Shower enclosures, for example, are seen as intrusions in the space. This is not a style conducive to the fingerprints of family living. The absence of textural contrasts can be disconcerting. In this minimalist bathroom, the addition of a mirrored wall visually doubles the size of a tiny space. The basin appears to float off the wall, giving an ethereal quality.

3. NEW SCANDINAVIAN

An open-plan design, focusing on light and space, with a combination of blond woods and smooth white walls, gives this style its modern Swedish sensibility. Furniture is restrained in style and the bath and basin are white. This concept is an ideal alternative to the more traditional ensuite. Here, a bath space is integrated into the main bedroom. The bedroom area is defined by sisal carpeting which meets with the tiles of the wet area. A Philippe Starck tub and Tasmanian oak cupboards complete the contemporary look.

4. HOTEL CHIC

A grand hotel style tugs at the senses. It's a look that relies on a layering of textural elements to increase the feeling of luxury. Glass, wood, mirror, marble, stone and extravagantly shaped fittings align with the deepest bath possible. Go for the five-star look with space to read or watch television, from the bath, of course. This bed/bath suite has a built-in basin and dressing table which doubles as a writing desk. The shower is concealed behind a translucent glass door. Limestone covers the floor and supports the bath.

5. ART DECO

Bathrooms in an Art Deco style have a glamorous, romantic appeal. Their attraction lies in the dynamic use of tiles, distinctive curvy shapes, bevelled mirrors and chrome accessories. While Art Deco bathrooms have a serious look about them, they are also elegant. Here, colours of mint and black set the theme for an Art Deco-inspired bathroom. The starting point was a curvaceous vanity unit edged in shiny metal. Round mirrors and wall sconces have authentic appeal.

4

5

bathroomstyle

6. SIMPLY ZEN

Reduced to the bare minimum, the Zen-inspired bathroom reflects a belief that the process of getting clean is a sensual, rejuvenating experience made more pleasurable if there is a vista of trees to gaze upon. There is a blurred line between inside and out, which makes this kind of bathroom a possibility for the rear of a house and where privacy is not at risk. The scale of this room is sympathetic to the rest of the house, where open-plan living and sharp but simple lines are evident.

7. EUROPEAN

This style has a strong bond with tradition yet it is essentially a modern space where the focus is on a luxurious bathing experience. The French-influenced look blends heirlooms and antiques with designer pieces in all-white surroundings, warmed by a dark wood floor. Integral to the style is the D-shaped pedestal basin, older-style taps and ornately framed wall mirror. If you have the room, consider it as a fashionable alternative to a separate bathroom. This design integrates bathroom facilities into a bedroom, with an enormous spa bath complete with overhead shower nozzle.

8. NEW HERITAGE

This is the style of a collector with a penchant for period architecture and antiques. Richly detailed, it puts an appreciation of tradition into a modern context. Designed to complement a Federation house, the style of this classic bathroom was influenced by those iconic 1980s television series, *Dallas* and *Dynasty*. Mirror, marble, gold-plated taps, etched glass and a generous tub create a mood reminiscent of a grand European residence.

bathroomcolour

Most of the colour in a bathroom comes from its structure – from the bath itself, the basin and the tiles on the wall. It's crucial that you decide on a colour scheme at the initial stages of planning a new bathroom. But having said that, the fastest and most stylish way to update an old bathroom is with a coat of paint on the walls, and bath towels and accessories in a new colour. And whether you want to use the bathroom to energise or to relax and restore spirits, there is a colour scheme to match the mood.

1. COMPLEMENTARY WITH A SECONDARY COLOUR

Pale golden yellow makes a great backdrop to the more dramatic colours used in the elaborate tiling of a Moroccan styled bathroom. Blue-based teal green, the secondary colour, is the dominant accent and complements the warmer yellow.

2. COMPLEMENTARY WITH PRIMARIES

Yellow and blue give a bathroom a great atmosphere. These primary colours make a very balanced partnership as the colours lie directly opposite each other on the colour wheel (see page 24). Remember, yellow works best with a blue of the same depth.

3. RELATED COLOURS

A harmonious, calming, yet optimistic mood is created when you combine colours that sit next to each other on the colour wheel, like blue and green (see page 24). Here, turquoise, which is a mix of blue and green, reveals its universal appeal in bathrooms.

4. EARTHY NEUTRALS

The natural colours of stone bring a sense of restrained luxury to a bathroom. Marble tile in a tonal striation of rich, earthy colour is the signature of this elegant ensuite. Brown is a combination of many colours, so it works with almost any other hue. Here, however, clean white and touches of black have been used for a crisp effect.

5. NEUTRALS WITH AN ACCENT COLOUR

White plus wood is a fashionable combination for contemporary bathrooms. The warmth and texture of the honey-toned wood used here help temper white's austere and often impersonal ambience.

1. Black and white tiles sharpen the brilliance of hot hues like pink and orange.
2. Texture and colour soften hard bathroom surfaces.
3. Tinted glass brings its own ethereal hint of colour.
4. Fresh flowers and toiletries combine delightful fragrance with a discreet colour splash.
5. Colour does not need to be vibrant to make an impact.

PLANNING

Attitudes to using colour in the bathroom have changed over the years. The glossy black and mustard tiling and avocado toilet suites of the Art Deco era, for example, were an attempt to revoke the sterility of the all-white bathroom. And whereas the white bathroom of Victorian times spoke of cleanliness and hygiene, today's desire for a white scheme stems from a need for tranquillity.

A bathroom requires the same kind of planning that a kitchen does to make the colour, texture and pattern of surfaces work to create a cohesive whole. Matching your collection of paint chips and material samples to their position on a floor plan will help you determine a good-looking colour scheme.

Colour comes from the materials with which you surface the walls and floor. It also comes from the fittings and from applied decoration, like paint to walls and woodwork, window treatments, cabinets, door hardware, glass and accessories.

Tile is the most frequently used medium to bring colour to a bathroom, and it is the trend to take the tiles, often mosaic, right to the ceiling. Used in this way, a single colour can dominate a scheme. On the other hand, in today's family bathroom, texture is a big style-setter and it is used in combination with colour to make a distinctive scheme. An example of this is a scheme focused around the neutrals of cream, coffee and brown, where hard surfaces such as stone or marble are matched with recycled wood and frosted or colour-backed glass.

COLOUR FOR MOOD

Decide how you will use the space because colour can help create the right mood to enhance your bathing experience. Serene or stimulating? The choice is yours. If you want to take long relaxing baths in the evening, then a calming scheme would be more appropriate than one designed for a family responding to the wake-up call of an early-morning shower.

Restful/calming The most soothing colours for bathrooms are those that relate, like blue and green which sit close to each other on the colour wheel. Aqua with pale lime or periwinkle with spearmint will achieve a contemporary look.

The neutrals are also restful because they are easy on the eye.

Energising/revitalising A complementary colour scheme, like blue and yellow, is an ideal combination for a family or children's bathroom, where action is more important than relaxation. White can be dynamic because of its light-enhancing qualities, yet a little impersonal. However, when textures from stone, wood and wicker are added, the all-white bathroom becomes softer and more sensual.

127

bathroom**storage**

For a bathroom to function like clockwork, it must have good storage. This will ensure that a towel is within easy reach when you emerge from the bath or shower, the toothpaste is discreetly hidden, and the first-aid kit is instantly accessible should accidents strike. To create a safe, streamlined and efficient space, storage has to address the specific needs of each of the room's functional zones, centred around the bath, shower, wash basin and toilet. As the location of these fixtures is generally dictated by the existing plumbing, it makes sense to decide on where they're going before you start planning your storage.

BUILDING IN STORAGE

The size of the bathroom will obviously dictate what you can store there. A family bathroom will need storage for everything from nappies and bath toys to toiletries, make-up and shaving gear. Medicines should be kept in a locked cabinet or out of children's reach. In a small bathroom, you may have to stow extra towels and other supplies elsewhere.

Architectural modifications may win you more storage space. As well as delineating zones within a bathroom, a free-standing wall can incorporate alcoves and shelves to serve the spaces on either side. A stepped bathing platform gives you a

vehicle for display and storage, and a place to kneel when bathing a child. Wash basins set into a vanity cupboard provide scope for storage, while a wall of floor-to-ceiling cupboards could provide the bulk of your storage needs in a clean sweep.

Generally, the vanity cupboard will provide the bulk of the storage in a bathroom. You can make the cupboard work harder by fitting accessories such as wire racks, sliding shelves and bins.

Kitchen storage units, as long as they're water-resistant, adapt well to the bathroom. Particle board, whether it's finished in laminate or polyurethane, should be a highly moisture resistant (HMR) grade.

1. Wall-mounted cupboards and basin keep the look clear and uncluttered.
2. To deal with a lack of wall space, a chrome towel ladder is fitted to the bath surround, where it doubles as a screen for the toilet.
3. Open timber shelving and a mobile trolley are a flexible and attractive storage solution.
4. Wall-hung fittings enhance a feeling of space in this bathroom. Separate units define the washing/shaving and make-up zones. The basin unit is fitted with doors and shelves, and its neighbour has space-efficient drawers.

1

2

3

4

5

6

7

8

1. Baskets provide suitably airy storage for the towel supplies in a washroom.

2. Wall-mounted, adjustable shaving mirrors help keep a vanity top free of clutter.

3. Beech joinery conceals all but the towels in this bathroom. A tiled ledge and hanging rack store shower essentials.

4. A lab-style sink tops this sleek cabinet, which is raised off the floor to enhance the room's spatial flow. A recessed roll-holder serves the adjacent toilet, which slots neatly into the alcove created by the cabinet and the wall.

5. Test-tube vases set into a timber shelf and filled with flowers bring a sunny feel to a powder room under the stairs. Hand-towels with eyelets slot neatly onto simple chrome hooks.

6. A mobile trolley means bathing essentials can be moved from bath to shower easily. The woven basket is a convenient hiding spot for clothes and used towels.

7. A slim, floor-to-ceiling cupboard neatly divides twin washing zones and keeps bathroom clutter out of sight. The space at the top houses an extractor fan.

8. A built-in unit packs a lot of storage into a small space, with deep shelves for towels and accessories, drawers for make-up and toiletries, and a vanity space for grooming. A strip of pebbled tile provides textural relief against a spread of white cupboard doors.

Be a little cautious about using timber in a bathroom. It's liable to warp in high humidity, so the room must be properly ventilated. The moisture-resistant properties of cedar or celery-top pine make them the most suitable to use but, as with any timber, they should be sealed on all sides prior to construction.

Timber veneers are claimed to be more stable than solid wood in moist environments, but they should always be treated with at least three coats of polyurethane or a similar sealer to ensure a durable, water-resistant finish.

TAMING TOWELS

Be prepared to give over considerable cupboard space to towel storage in a typical family bathroom. Space for storing towels, whether in current use or a back-up supply, should always be a priority. A laundry basket for used towels is also a good idea.

Towels must be within easy reach of the bath and basin, for obvious reasons of safety and comfort, and to avoid pools of water on the floor. Where children share the bathroom, towel hooks or rails must be at a height they can reach.

Heated towel rails, either electric or connected to a central heating system, will prevent the bathtime horror of cold, damp towels. Alternatively, fit a towel rail near a wall-mounted heater. You can also keep towels toasty by fitting cabinets with a heating element connected to the hot-water pipes. Avoid open storage where condensation could be a problem.

INCIDENTAL STORAGE

The intimate nature of bathroom rituals should be safeguarded by adequate concealed storage, ideally with separate areas for each member of the household. Storage boxes with individual compartments will keep all manner of bottles, tubes, jars and cartons tidy and in one place. Open shelving should be reserved for items that look good, and the rest stowed away.

Put the walls to work, making use of the dead space above the toilet for slim shelving (but leave some clearance so you can easily remove the cistern lid for maintenance). Install a narrow shelf along the top of a tiled or wood-panelled area. Shallow shelves are suitable for toiletries, with deeper ones for bulky items such as towels, tissues and toilet rolls.

Fix hooks, racks and rails to doors and inside cupboards, and use suction-mounted accessories where walls have to remain intact. Corner fixtures are a sensible choice for a small space, and a mobile trolley can be used to share resources between two or more zones.

STORAGE IDEAS
- As well as hanging space for towels, include a rail for face washers within easy reach of the bath. Soap and other bath essentials should also be close at hand. A bath rack can solve storage problems easily. To ease the transition from splash-around kids' space to a relaxing pampering zone, have somewhere to hide the rubber ducks and squeaky bath toys – a net bag works well.
- A mirror-fronted wall cabinet positioned above the wash basin adds to the functionality of this hard-working space.
- Like baths, showers must have somewhere to store soap and shampoo. Built-in ledges or wall-mounted racks are useful here. A corner unit will make less gains on the space, and accessories in polished chrome or plastic-coated wire will stand up to regular soaking.
- A cupboard in the wall space above the toilet is a natural place for bulk toilet-roll storage as well as reading material for closet bookworms.

bathroom walls&floors

When it comes to bathroom surfaces, practicality rules. The choice of finish for walls and floors has to be sensible and safe. Surfaces must cope with constant steam and water, yet be easy to live with. Ceramic, stone, timber and glass are happy playing in the splash zone, so long as you treat them right.

1. This bathroom borrows an idea from old country washhouses, using ripple iron on the walls instead of tiles. It's waterproof and can look old world or cutting edge, depending on the accessories. **2.** Tiles lend themselves to a graphic treatment. In this simple but very effective scheme, black and aquamarine tiles with white grouting create a strong impact.

WALLS

In bathrooms, the area around the shower must be completely waterproof and walls next to the bath and basin should be water-resistant, at least. Elsewhere, walls must be able to handle condensation. This is no place for unsealed plaster, plain wallpaper or unfinished wood, as they'll be damaged by the humidity.

Lay a solid base by fitting waterproof lining board in the bathroom's wet areas, with flashing to the corners. This helps stop moisture migrating from the shower to the rest of the room, where it can do damage. If you're planning to have an open shower, or 'wet room', it's necessary to make the whole room waterproof.

So what to put on top of that waterproof lining board? Ceramic or glass tiles are waterproof and easy to clean, but make sure the grouting is waterproof, too, to stop moisture seeping through. Stone tiles, marble and limestone offer a luxurious finish, but should be sealed to make them less porous.

If the thought of scrubbing tiles or grouting leaves you cold, you may prefer to have prefinished, wet-area panelling in your shower zone, or even glass bricks to let in the sunlight.

Away from the shower, things don't have to be totally waterproof, although you may want to extend the same finish for a more unified look. Tongue-and-groove panelling (properly sealed) and paint are practical choices for the walls, but add an anti-mould agent to the paint before it goes on, or choose one specially formulated for bathrooms. If you would like wallpaper, choose one with a vinyl finish and use a fungicidal adhesive.

Remember, bathroom walls should be frequently wiped down to combat mould, so make sure that the surfaces you choose are easy to clean.

PRACTICAL BATHROOM FLOORS

Splashes, spilt lotions, hair dye and nail polish are all part of life for bathroom floors. Safety is a major concern, too, as many accidents happen in this part of the home. But don't feel restricted in your choices – there's a surprising range of materials that can do the job. And as bathrooms tend to be more compact than other rooms in the home, you can choose a more luxurious option without breaking the bank. Tumbled marble tiles and limestone are all affordable when you're buying only a small quantity. However if your budget is tight, opt for large rather than small tiles, as you need fewer to cover the same area of floor. Just remember that flooring in a bathroom must be waterproof, non-slip (even when it's wet) and warm underfoot.

1. Timber isn't forbidden in bathrooms. Here, toughened glass walls team with weatherboards, treated with two coats of paint in a satin finish. The floor is blackbutt boards, set 5mm apart. Water drains through to a tray. The owners asked that the floorboards be left unsealed so that they'd weather naturally.

2. A bathroom for four boys is no place for sensitive surfaces, and these heavily streaked marble tiles have the advantage of disguising soap marks. The floor is well sealed American oak, which harmonises with the Tasmanian oak ceiling.

3. Different sized tiles have been used to eye-catching effect. Large limestone tiles surround a spa bath, with the bath itself finished in darker coloured glass mosaics.

4. Several shades of white combine for the finishes in this bathroom.

5. Glass mosaic tiles in cool aquamarine, green and white make this bathroom feel like an underwater cave.

6. Ceramic tiles stretch to the ceiling in this room, creating a spatial illusion of extra height. But it's the bold terrazzo floor that really demands attention.

7. This ensuite blends into the bedroom, with a mirrored wall behind the vanity reflecting the rest of the room.

HARD FLOORS

Ceramic and mosaic tiles, marble and limestone are favourites for bathroom floors. They're all hard-wearing and water-proof (if they're properly sealed), but their surfaces tend to be cold in winter. If you can, install underfloor heating to take off the chilly edge. Rubber-backed mats will also warm bare feet.

Stick to matt-finish floor tiles and marble and stone with a tumbled or honed finish, as super-glossy tiles and highly polished stone are slippery when wet. Remember, too, that stone will have to be sealed to prevent it staining.

If you want terrazzo in the bathroom, make sure there's a non-slip aggregate added to the mixture – terrazzo and soap are a notoriously slippery combination.

Terracotta tile looks beautiful in the bathroom, but it must be sealed profes-sionally and regularly, or it will soak up stains and absorb odours.

RESILIENT FLOORS

If you'd prefer a slightly softer feel under-foot, try cushioned vinyl, linoleum or studded rubber flooring. They're warmer than ceramic or stone and easier to change if you tire of the colour scheme. Sealed cork is also suitable for bathrooms.

Try to minimise joins where water can seep in; wide sheets may be more practi-cal here than rubber or vinyl in tile form.

TIMBER

Timber is a more limited choice in the bathroom, but so long as it is a water-resistant species and is properly sealed and maintained, it can work well. Take the same approach as for boat decks and finish the wood with marine varnish. You can even caulk between the boards. Timber gets a little slick when wet, though, so rubber-backed mats are a prudent addition to the scheme.

Bamboo flooring is another option. It has a similar look to wood, but with its denser grain it is naturally more water-resistant than timber.

CARPET

Carpet may be the ultimate in underfoot comfort, but it's not good in a family bathroom. All that steam and spilt sham-poo will make the jute backing rot, and damp fibres will leave a lingering odour.

That's not to say carpets are absolutely forbidden: in ornate ensuites, a fast-drying synthetic carpet is a reasonable option, just don't put it in the direct line of splash. Avoid fixing it wall-to-wall, as you may have to lift it to dry out at some point.

Sisal and coir aren't suitable for bath-rooms. Coir is prickly underfoot and expands when damp, while sisal shrinks. Both also show water marks, unless they're stain-protected, so it's best to keep them away from the wet.

bathroom lighting&windows

The bathroom demands an adaptable lighting scheme. While effective task lighting is essential over the mirror, the rest of the space benefits from a softer, more subdued treatment. An overlit room filled with reflective surfaces jars the senses, so tone down the glow with a dimmer switch. Add a few candles and you'll be meditating in the bath in no time. Don't ignore daylight: the bathroom is where you greet the day, so open it to the sunshine and fresh air and you'll embrace the morning on a more positive note.

WINDOWS

Daylight is a welcome visitor to the bathroom. As well as putting you in a good mood for the start of the day, it also helps to dry out the moisture in the room. Windows and skylights bring in the sunshine, but how do you open the bathroom to the light and air, yet still retain some privacy? One solution is to set fixed windows high in the wall; called clerestory windows, these allow in light but avoid giving the neighbours a view.

Another idea is to fit the windows with textured or frosted glass, so that sunshine streams through but prying eyes are kept at bay. Glass bricks are also an option.

Of course, sometimes you will simply want to dress the window. Blinds or shutters are a better choice than curtains in a bathroom, as moisture makes fabrics limp and prone to mildew. But if you want curtains, choose lightweight weaves that will dry quickly, or make your own drapes from shower-curtain fabric.

1. If you live in a warm climate, take advantage of this aspect and open your bathroom to the great outdoors. Here, an adjustable sliding shutter can be pulled across to give privacy or pushed back to afford views of the garden and beyond.
2. The serene air of a Japanese bathhouse translates well to a contemporary bathroom. A sliding glass door, etched at the top for privacy, opens to the side passage and brings in abundant light. Off-white limestone tiles on the walls and floor contrast with the dark wood vanity, which is furnished with two sleek washing planes, moulded from Corian. Overhead halogen spots suffuse through a translucent panel, while lighting recessed behind the mirror provides even illumination for applying make-up.

1. There's no need for mechanical assistance to clear the steam in this bathroom. An arrangement of frosted glass louvres and angled glazed panels promotes good ventilation and also makes a compact space seem bigger.

2. Moisture-resistant, stained cedar venetian blinds address the privacy issue. Downlights provide an even light that is reflected off the marble tiles, making them appear even more luxurious. An illuminated cabinet contains fragrances and other toiletries, creating a focal point in the room.

3. Contemplating a garden scene from your bath is a Japanese tradition that the Western world is happy to embrace. This ensuite has been relocated so the bather can open sliding windows to a view of the ever-changing ocean. Privacy isn't a big issue here, although a simple roman blind is there when needed. Limestone tiles in a dark sand tone are used on the floor, walls and around the bath to bring an earthy serenity to the scheme.

4. Timber venetians dress a platoon of narrow windows in this bathroom. The blinds can be angled to let in light while still preserving the occupant's privacy. The stone tiles and gloss-finished cupboards mean that every shard of light is bounced around the space and made to work hard. Spotlights over the mirror are angled for best effect and an exhaust fan boosts ventilation.

5. A deep window is fitted with an austrian blind made from a semi-sheer cotton fabric. Being light and filmy, the cotton will dry more quickly than heavier fabrics and be less prone to mildew. Making up a swag from shower-curtain material is another practical solution.

5

VENTILATION

Fresh air is essential for a pleasant bathroom atmosphere, but often it's not given the attention it deserves. There's nothing more depressing than washing in a dark, damp room, where the moisture hangs around all day.

An open window is the simple solution, when privacy is not an issue. Sash-hung windows are a better option than sliding windows, as they allow you to leave the top open for ventilation. Louvre windows can be partially opened to let through a breeze. Most bathrooms, however, need the help of an exhaust fan to remove all the condensation.

EXHAUST FANS
Exhaust fans are a very effective way to banish steam and moisture from the bathroom. Make sure you buy one with enough power for the size of your bathroom. Calculate the volume of the room in cubic metres (multiply its depth by its height and width), then choose an exhaust fan that can change the same volume of air a minimum of 10 to a maximum of 20 times an hour. In bathrooms with no windows, the exhaust fan should be wired to switch on with the light.

bathroomlighting&windows

A PRACTICAL LIGHTING PLAN

For a good bathroom lighting scheme:

• Plan for task lighting around the vanity basin. You want an even light that avoids harsh, unflattering shadows. It should not be too bright, either, otherwise you may overdo your make-up. The Hollywood-star arrangement of tungsten globes around a mirror works very well, especially as tungsten light enhances skin tones. But if that seems too extravagant, have wall lights on each side of the mirror, or one light above the glass, either mounted in a recess in the ceiling or behind a pelmet. This will prevent those nasty shadows. Some ready-made mirrored cabinets come with lighting built-in on each side.

• Rather than pendant lights, use spotlights or a series of recessed downlights to provide ambient light in the bathroom; they're neater and safer. Light bulbs can short-circuit when damp, so you should avoid fittings that expose a bare bulb.

• Fit a dimmer switch so lights can be adjusted to suit your mood. It's safest to locate the dimmer switch outside the bathroom so it's not affected by steam.

• Some fluorescent tubes have a greenish cast to their light that makes a white-tiled bathroom look particularly cold and uninviting. Halogen downlights or tungsten bulbs are a better option.

• Remember that light fittings, light switches and power points should be fitted at least 50cm away (horizontally) from the shower area, bath or basin, and 1.2 metres above. For safety, light fittings should never be installed directly over the shower. Waterproof spotlights, which are totally sealed, can be installed closer to splash zones, but always ask an electrician, builder or architect for advice.

• Make provision for those night-time treks to the toilet by installing a low-wattage night light in the bathroom, or go hi-tech and install an infrared movement detector which turns on lights automatically so you don't have to fumble for the light switch.

1. In this bathroom, several slim windows let in natural light, with an etched panel across the middle of the glass providing privacy. Mosaic tiles stretch from the floor to the ceiling and generous mirrors reflect the sunshine.

2. Small square windows are fixed high in rammed-earth walls to keep this ensuite very private. Decorative wall sconces with glass shades complement the colour scheme and provide an effective light for the mirror.

3. Translucent glass louvres let through subtropical breezes and provide welcome side lighting for the vanity area. Downlights take over at night, but are angled so they give a flattering light and don't cast shadows.

bathroomfixtures&fittings

There have been ground-breaking changes in bathroom design. Basins have morphed into elongated washing planes and bowl-shaped vessels, and the touch-free bathroom, where sensors determine when taps flow and toilets flush, is becoming a reality. Bathroom fixtures are thought of as long-term investments, so be wary of choosing exotic finishes or radical shapes if you're not sure their appeal will last the distance. White is perennially popular. It complements both traditional and modern designs and is immune to the whims of fashion. Apart from the cost benefits of selecting standard white, you can combine items from different manufacturers and replace or add to fixtures more easily.

1. A 'floating' glass basin was custom-designed for this small guest bathroom to minimise visual intrusion and be in context with the room's contemporary lines.
2. This large open space is demarcated into zones for sleeping, watching television and bathing. A Victorian-style bath takes on a sculptural form, positioned on a honed limestone platform. The cubicles behind are for the toilet and shower.

THE BATH

Today, the bath is a place to relax and unwind, rather than somewhere to simply scrub up and make a quick exit, so it needs to be designed for comfort.

The average precast bath is 150-180cm long, 70-80cm wide and 40cm deep. There's an interesting range of shapes and sizes that goes beyond the standard white rectangle, from corner and freestanding designs to sunken baths.

Bath surrounds can be custom-built platforms or tiled enclosures designed to include storage for soaps and towels.

If space demands a small bath, select one at least 45cm deep so you can still enjoy a soak. If a bath will be used by children or an elderly person, choose a design with a grab rail and non-slip surface.

Materials will determine the durability and the price of your bath. A pressed metal design with a porcelain enamel finish is generally the cheapest option, but is prone to chipping, is a poor insulator, and is twice the weight of an acrylic equivalent. Acrylic baths tend to be more costly, but are warm to the touch, better insulators, and come in many shapes and colours. The traditional enamel-coated cast-iron bath is more durable and heat-insulating than pressed metal designs, but its considerable weight may prevent you installing it in an upstairs room.

bathroomfixtures&fittings

1. The conical basin and floor-mounted gooseneck tap in this striking bathroom look suitably sculptural. The mirror conceals a slim cupboard for bathroom essentials.
2. A mosaic-lined 'lounge' and massaging showerhead turn a bathroom into a day spa.
3. A sliding rail fitting and hand-held shower allow for smooth adjustments in height and direction of flow.
4. A frosted glass vessel basin and sleek mixer tap poised on a simple travertine marble bench create a refined setting in which to wash hands.
5. A small laboratory sink is perfect for a compact guest bathroom.
6. Floor-to-ceiling panels of translucent glass maximise light while safeguarding privacy. A frameless glass shower screen keeps this small bathroom looking spacious.
7. A carved stone basin, whimsical tiles and display niches create a room where romantic allusions win over pure utility.
8. Period-style lever taps look great in modern settings.
9. This bathroom exudes a Zen-like calm and makes a pleasure of the bathing ritual. The unconventional fittings include these highly sculptural washing planes, paired with elegant tapware.

A deep, wooden tub instantly conjures the hedonism of a Japanese bathhouse, but it's a luxury, even in Japan, where plastic is now more common. Wooden baths, traditionally in Japanese cypress or Chinese black pine, must be replaced periodically as the wood disintegrates from prolonged contact with water.

SPA BATHS
Before splashing out on the luxury of a spa bath, check your hot-water system has enough capacity to fill it; most require 120-160 litres to function. Look for designs that are shaped for comfort, with built-in lounger seats and jets positioned to reach parts of your body that hold tension (the neck, shoulders and upper back) and with safety features such as non-slip bases, built-in steps and hand-rails. Acrylic spas are more popular than fibreglass, as they come in a wider range of colours and shapes.

BASINS
The basin is available in wall-hung, pedestal, semi-recessed or recessed designs, and can be made of porcelain, stone, stainless steel or glass.

The wall-hung basin is the simplest and generally cheapest option, while recessed or partly recessed designs are built into a base unit, either a bench or cupboard, that conceals the plumbing. While visually bulky compared to pedestal and wall-mounted designs, built-in basins are best in compact bathrooms, as

storage can be included in the base section. Vessel basins sit on top of a bench to show off their designer shapes.

If you want twin basins, leave about 20cm between them so they can be used comfortably at the same time.

SHOWERS
The shower has become a serious pampering zone in its own right, with an assortment of shower settings to relax or invigorate as required.

While it's possible to attach multi-functional showerheads to most fittings, you'll need to check whether your water pressure is adequate for their operation. Hand-held showerheads on long hoses are great for cleaning the shower as well as small children, while a shower attached to a sliding rail can be adjusted to suit a range of heights. Fixed ceiling- or wall-mounted showerheads give a clean appearance but lack the flexibility of hand-held or adjustable designs.

In the pursuit of streamlined design, shower zones are increasingly left open, forming so-called 'wet rooms', or invisibly defined by frameless glass shower screens. Framed glass screens are much cheaper, with pivot-door models simpler to use than three-panel sliding models.

If you're buying a pre-fabricated one-piece shower module in acrylic or fibreglass, check that it will fit through doors and openings en route to the bathroom. As with the bath, the floor should be slip-resistant and a handrail is recommended.

NUMBERS TO KNOW

• **Bath**	Allow an area 110 x 70cm alongside the bath and 220cm headroom above (less if the bath is sunken).
• **Basins**	Leave a 90cm space in front and 20cm on each side.
• **Toilets**	Allow 80cm of space in front and 20cm on each side.
• **Showers**	Cubicles enclosed on three sides should be at least 90 x 90cm; for unenclosed showers, allow 90 x 80cm of space. Have a 90 x 90cm space in front for access.

1

TOILETS

The introduction of one-piece toilets in the 1960s, with their integrated pan and cistern, brought a welcome sleekness to the bathroom. However, the two-piece unit, being cheaper, is still around.

In general terms, elongated bowls are more sanitary, higher-seated designs more comfortable, and round bowls ideal for small spaces. Hiding the cistern in the wall recess (if you have one) gives a more streamlined look, but you must allow access for maintenance purposes.

Saving water is another concern. The newer 3-litre/6-litre dual-flush units use up to 70 per cent less water than conventional 11-litre cisterns, and are mandatory for new homes in many areas.

TAPS

Like other bathroom fittings, taps continue to take on more aerodynamic, sculptural forms. A cross-over from the kitchen, the mixer tap is increasingly a bathroom standard. It's easier to use and clean, and generally more water-efficient.

Ceramic discs, a quite recent innovation superseding traditional washers or jumper valves, give the mixer tap its smooth, effortless action and extended drip-free service, as well as eliminating water hammer (banging in the pipes).

Taps can be wall- or vanity-mounted, or plumbed through holes in the bath or basin. Designs will need to be compatible with existing plumbing and the style of bath or basin, and should feel comfortable in your hand.

For safety and convenience, shower taps should be vertically aligned to one side of the showerhead so they can be accessed without having to reach under the potentially hot spray of water.

You should fit aerators and/or flow-restrictors to basin taps to conserve water, and temperature limiting devices if children use the bathroom.

A swan or gooseneck tap is good for a basin in a bathroom-cum-laundry, as it gives berth for filling a bucket.

While there's a wealth of tap finishes available, the hardness of the water in your area may limit your options. Chrome and heavy-duty white or coloured plastic are safe for hard-water areas, while brass and gold-plated finishes are likely to tarnish.

1. A combination of fixed and hopper windows provides a framed view from the bath without sacrificing privacy. Twin vanities, flanked by convenience benches in white marble, provide 'his and her' storage, supplemented with a central unit with shallow drawers for storing bathroom sundries, a mirror and a shaver socket. Twin cupboards recessed in the wall above each vanity ensure that everything has its place.
2. A laboratory-style sink serves as a wash basin in this small bathroom. Taps are set into the mirror so that it cleverly doubles as a splashback for the basin. The toilet's concealed cistern helps contribute to the uncluttered look.
3. Twin vessel basins rest on the marble top of a compact vanity in rock-maple veneer. The satin chrome taps are matched to the cupboard handles to keep the look clean and consistent.
4. Pebbles set in tile form a textural contrast to the sleek geometry of an integrated porcelain basin. With its generous surface for resting soap and other items, it serves as a space-conscious vanity top for a compact bathroom.
5. A simple pedestal conceals the downpipe of a Roman-shaped washing vessel.

2 3

4 5

bedroom

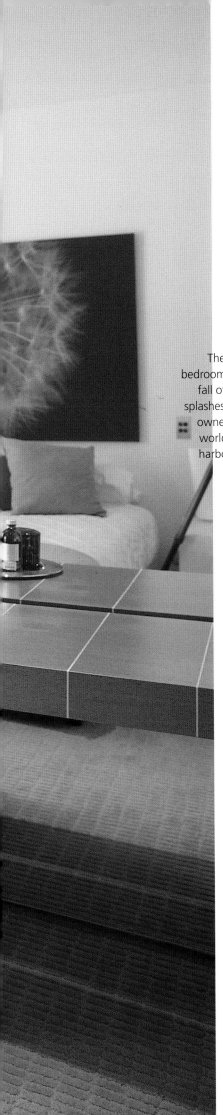

The rhythm of this apartment bedroom is marked by the rise and fall of natural light and random splashes of citrus colour. Here, the owner can retreat into a private world, or embrace the dazzling harbour view from the balcony.

The bedroom used to be the most undervalued room in the house, yet we rely on its existence to get through our lives. Today's bedroom should be a physical and emotional retreat from the busy world. It's a modern habit, however, to spend an inordinate amount of time and money getting the home's practical zones just right, while failing to pay enough attention to the only space that is truly yours. The bedroom is much more than a night room; it's your own domain where you can do and be whatever you like. It's a profoundly personal space, and in a busy family home, where the action level comes close to matching that of an airport terminal, that counts for a lot.

bedroomzones

The room once mainly thought of as a space in which to put the bed has become the restorative centre for both body and mind, an oasis of peace and relaxation and an environment given over to pursuing personal pleasures. In a family home, that means the primary escape route for parents hankering after solitude and freedom from household chores and the ferrying of noisy children. Planning the perfect bedroom is all about analysing individual needs within the existing space, and determining what furnishings you would like to include in that space. So, if watching a video, listening to soft music or surfing the internet late at night are activities you enjoy in your private world, then plan accordingly.

1. PLEASURE

The bathroom may merge discreetly with the bedroom to create a true pleasure zone. Less is indeed more in this Eastern-inspired bedroom. The space is smooth, clutter-free, and there is a feeling of sensuality and enticement in an arrangement that is ideally suited to an adult's retreat.

2. COMFORT

In today's modern bedroom, there's a risk of trying to cram in too many functions. The result can be a space cluttered with superfluous furnishings. Instead, put the focus back on the bed and streamline items to allow for the luxury of space. This bedroom opens to the living area through sliding glass doors which are pushed apart to reveal a view, from the bed, of the Sydney Harbour Bridge.

3. QUIET REFLECTION

It's important to make a place away from the bed for reading and for perhaps writing letters or entries in a diary. A sofa table or credenza placed at the end of a bed maximises floor space; it also offers the perfect spot for keeping house keys, letters and jewellery visible. In this small bedroom, an antique side table does admirable duty as a writing desk.

5 **6**

4. BEDSIT

The spacious bedsitting room with elegant sofas and a place to put a teacup or martini glass harks at a more gracious, opulent, Hollywood-movie era. But in fact, it has its roots further back in history. Up until the 18th century, people ate, entertained and slept in the one room. So nothing is new, simply more refined, and today more appropriate to our modern lifestyle. A theatrical platform bed in this well-appointed bedroom is the centrepiece in a suite of comfort and style.

5. INDOOR/OUTDOOR

There's nothing like abundant natural light for creating a healthy atmosphere in a bedroom. Where possible, consider the best aspect for sunshine and open up the room to the outdoors. This will extend the social life of your bedroom by offering a special spot to relax, have breakfast or a lazy read of the weekend papers. You will find that you feel permanently on holiday. Here, cedar-framed doors push back to reveal a tropical-style bedroom with a sunny disposition and breezy outlook.

6. MULTI-PURPOSE

An adaptable bedroom that can ease smoothly from study into guest mode is a valuable asset. In the modern bedroom, a study desk converts to a writing desk and a divan or daybed works just as well as a comfortable couch. In a city townhouse where space is at a premium, the concept of a study-cum-guestroom works perfectly.

bedroomstyle

The bedroom has no stereotype, which makes it by far the most interesting room to decorate. The bedroom does not have to echo the decorative style of any other space and, for most people, it satisfies an inherent longing for the one room you can decorate exclusively for personal pleasure. If you live in a family home, the main bedroom may be the only room where adults rule and kids' toys and family clutter are banished. This is one room where you have a free hand to relax the rules; no copybook style but your own. Besides, the atmosphere is more likely to appear authentic if it has subtly evolved over time.

1. GALLERY

Art is a way of making sense of the world and what better place to display personal artworks and creations than the private realm of the bedroom. This style embraces simplicity and tranquillity, with a minimalist approach to furnishings. It is an all-day room with an all-day bed, creatively inspired and designed.

2. BOHEMIAN

Flamboyant fabrics in contrasting textures and outrageous patterns set against smooth, cool metal give this style its funky flavour. Retro shapes and 'look-at-me' colours are key elements of this decidedly young-at-heart look. Everyday items can be easily transformed into special features by positioning them in the right spot. It is a style that expresses great originality and artistic flair.

3. MODERN COUNTRY

This look offers an accessible vision of understated decorating where colour and pattern are used informally. But it is the shape and scale of elements which give the depth that is so often lacking in modern, minimalist rooms. The well-bred check dashed with lots of white adds freshness to this lively take on country.

4. HIP HOTEL

Replicating at home the chic style of a ritzy city hotel room is a dream for many travellers. Tonal colour, crisp white bedlinen, plump pillows, designer furniture and minimal pattern are what makes this style so desirable. Yet dismiss all thoughts of this look if the kids and family dog or cat treat your bedroom as their morning playroom.

5. TROPICAL HIDEAWAY

A Japanese-inspired private retreat in the centre of a lush tropical garden has immense appeal as the perfect escape route to relaxation. With this look, traditional Eastern cultural influences are reinterpreted for Western ideals. Fabrics like ikat and batik are perfect for casual bedcovers, but the one requisite for comfort is the ubiquitous mosquito net.

4

5

6

7

6. BOUDOIR

Romantic bedrooms are all about opulent splendour and sumptuous textures. Close the door, draw the silk curtains and another world awaits in surroundings punctuated by French antiques, sophisticated ornamentation and decadent detailing. Colour is a rich play of neutrals to offset the highlights of gold and bronze.

7. DIVA

With its connotations of grandeur and sense of theatre, this style captures the essence of an era when bedrooms were the size of small apartments and their occupants would disappear behind closed doors with a stack of books and a bottle of vodka. This look is for those who love the elegance of European design and like sleeping in a four-poster bed. Here, there is a careful layering of old and new with a French silkscreen tapestry behind an Indonesian teak bed adorned with an Italian faux sable throw.

8. CLASSIC

This style draws reference from the English country house with its timeless, welcoming ambience. Never in or out of fashion, the look relies heavily on a beautifully detailed window treatment and an extravagant use of fine fabric. Detailing is characteristically pretty, but never fussy. You can almost smell the roses in this bedroom.

bedroomcolour

In the bedroom, the colour you need in the morning may not be the colour you want at night. There's no problem going to sleep in an aubergine, black or brown room, as these colours reflect little light. But waking in a sombre space can give you bad karma for the rest of the day. It's important to have colours that make you feel good whatever time you're in the bedroom. Think carefully about the mood you want to create and don't forget that pattern and texture will enhance your scheme.

1. COMPLEMENTARY USING SHADED COLOURS

Primary colours like blue and red are potentially exhausting to live with in a bedroom. But when pared back or 'dirtied' such as in this combination of raspberry and purple-toned blue, it's more restrained and restful. The white background acts as a binding agent while lime accents offer a contrast.

2. NEUTRALS

The lack of colour in white bedrooms means that texture takes centre stage. The overall effect is one of calm and tranquillity. Avoid trying to match whites because the blending of different shades, from porcelain to driftwood, is what creates the charm.

3. CLASSIC COMPLEMENTARY COLOURS

Red and green are complementary colours, opposite each other on the colour wheel (see page 24). Together they make a vibrant combination and feature throughout history as a popular choice for formal rooms. In a bedroom, however, be sure to use the red as an accent. Here, soft mossy green creates a restful, calming mood.

4. PASTELS

Pastels evoke images of painterly frescoes, are gentle on the eye and relaxing to live with night and day. Avoid the 'boring bedroom' syndrome by choosing chalky pastels, not those which are too bright or too sickly. Choose butter yellow, fondant pink, pistachio green and milky blue. Try painting a wall in graduated stripes of blue and green for a fresh look.

5. COMPLEMENTARY USING DARK COLOURS

Dark colours are those to which black has been added. The deep berry and wine-coloured shades like blueberry and claret make a dramatic play in today's modern bedroom. Accents of warm wood complement the hues. The depth of colour is determined by how much available natural light there is, so this bedroom becomes evocative and moody at night, and vibrant and soulful in the bright light of day.

bedroomcolour

1. Let texture and colour personalise your comfort zone.
2. Romance the bedroom with exquisite fabrics; shocking pink and raspberry red make electrifying accents.
3. Accessories bring a bedroom to life. Combine candles, bottles and potions for a pretty display.
4. Cherry red florals add lush highlights to a neutral scheme.
5. Use dazzling colour as an accent to liven up a white room. 'Clashing' colours like hot pinks and reds grab attention.

COLOUR FOR MOOD

You can create a scheme that makes you feel good by using a related or harmonious scheme for the background, such as blues and greens or whites and creams. Build up the drama with touches of energetic, physical colours such as scarlet, hot pink or orange for bedlinen and accessories. In this way, you can alter the atmosphere of the room to suit your mood. The most pleasurable, calming combinations, however, are those which lack sharp contrasts and are gentle on the eye.

White is a favourite and often a feminine choice for bedrooms. But a 'layered' monochromatic scheme around naturals such as white, cream, beige and grey is more desirable as it gives a rich tapestry of subtle colour changes. Certainly it crosses the gender barrier. The joy of a monochromatic scheme is that you can base your choice of colour solely on the effect it will have on your mood. To pull it off successfully, add liberal doses of texture in the furnishings. This creates a sensuous, sophisticated look with a wide appeal.

COLOUR IN ACCESSORIES

More than any other furnishing element, bedlinen brings a bedroom to life with colour, pattern and texture. Cushions, curtains and blinds, rugs, books, artworks and collectables add detail as well as colour, but it's the bed and its array of plump pillows, smoothly finished sheets and comforting quilt or blanket that sets both the decorative and colour theme. Even the timid decorator will revel in the opportunity to experiment with colours 'forbidden' in other areas of the home. Where else could you enjoy the juxtaposition of pink and red, orange and purple, aubergine and lime than in bedlinen designed to please and tease.

COLOUR THERAPY FOR THE BEDROOM

People often make the mistake of thinking all blues are soothing and relaxing. This is true to some extent and contributes to blue's reputation as the most popular colour for bedrooms. But a big expanse of dark blue is blatantly cold and unsuitable for a room with a shady aspect, where it can be depressing. If you have a quiet disposition or are prone to 'blue' moods, use a warm, red-based blue such as violet blue, lavender or french blue. Yellow is a stimulating colour that is best toned down for a bedroom so you don't have difficulty sleeping. Use a pale honey shade or primrose, and complement it with rose pink or pale blue. Shades of burgundy and plum are warming but give off less 'heat' than energising, dominating red which should be used only in small doses, either in a feature wall or accessories. Black, and white, make a fashion statement but be wary of their anti-social impact as hues for the bedroom. A good approach to living with an expanse of black is to 'balance' it with accents of a light and bright colour.

1

2 3

4 5

bedroom storage

Few bedrooms today are devoted solely to the purpose of sleep. The bedroom is where you usually store your clothes and personal items, dress and groom yourself and perhaps even wash. Yet for a bedroom to be conducive to sleep, it must be as clutter-free as possible. There should be few things to distract the eye or mind. Safeguarding this sense of serenity and calm owes much to the quality of the storage.

BESIDE THE BED

A bedside table, shelf or alcove is essential for keeping everyday items such as a reading light, alarm clock, drinking glass and perhaps a book and telephone close at hand. Tables, lamps and some form of book storage may even form part of the headboard design.

The table should be at a comfortable height, so you can glimpse the clock from your pillow, and large enough to accommodate all you need without causing a domino effect when you're switching on the lamp in the dark.

A surface 30cm across by 40cm deep is big enough for a clock, drinking glass and a book. Wall-mount the lamp and you'll have one less item on the table.

Storage beds, with integrated drawers, earn their keep in a tight space, providing a home for out-of-season quilts and blankets. Alternatively, invest in lidded storage boxes that slide underneath the bed.

STORING CLOTHES

A century ago, it was thought unhygienic to keep clothes in the bedroom. Yet today, much of the bedroom's storage is given over to clothes and accessories.

Hygienic or not, there are a lot of benefits in having a separate dressing room or walk-in wardrobe. As well as giving a bedroom more breathing space, it allows one person to dress while the other sleeps undisturbed. A dressing room should be at least 3.5 metres square and a walk-in wardrobe, 3 metres square.

Consider installing strip lights or halogen spots to any wardrobe space, to help you distinguish blacks from dark blues.

1. An alcove for books is a useful inclusion as it keeps the top of a unit clear.
2. These laminate shelves for stowing ties and shoes are tiered for viewing at a glance.
3. This sleek, full-height wardrobe makes the most efficient use of space.
4. Everything has its place and can be quickly accessed in this 'his and hers' walk-in dressing room. Hanging space is supplemented with pigeonholes for ties, belts and braces, slide-out shelves for shoes, and drawers for foldable clothes and underwear. Little-used items are stowed in shelves at the top.

1. A dressing room with Canadian rock-maple joinery doubles as an exercise space, with a chin-up bar straddling the cupboards.

2. An old carved wooden cabinet creates a focal point in an otherwise clean-lined bedroom, where the bulk of the storage is hidden within a walk-in wardrobe space. A freestanding metal valet readies an outfit for morning.

3. A gentle palette of earthy tones creates a restful mood in this guest bedroom, luxuriously equipped with a walk-in wardrobe/dressing room.

4. This walk-in dressing room has shop-fitting style cabinets to store sweaters, shirts and underwear. Concealed storage ensures clothes are protected from dust and daylight.

5. A shallow cupboard stores pairs of shoes on rods. It's a neat idea when there isn't room for drawers.

6. This streamlined room camouflages its storage. The veneer cupboard at the foot of the bed disguises a television, and behind the bedhead is space for clothes.

7. Shop-like open shelving makes for an attractive display of luggage and bags, ensuring they are instantly to hand. White melamine shelves blend with the walls and, combined with vertical chrome rods, give the shelving an overall feeling of lightness, appropriate for a bedroom. Lidded baskets keep paperwork under control.

8. Visible from the bedroom and bathroom, this well-appointed gentleman's dressing room is furnished to appear more as a living space, with antiques, a swagged blind and fine joinery. Floor-to-ceiling cupboards keep clothes and accessories out of sight, with closet interiors fitted out in economical laminate. A wicker basket makes a low-key laundry receptacle.

8

WARDROBES

The built-in wardrobe became popular in the 1970s and is now a mainstay of bedroom design. A floor-to-ceiling cupboard makes the most efficient use of space and, although costly to install, it is less distracting than a hotchpotch of mismatched, freestanding pieces.

Wardrobes should be at least 60cm deep to prevent clothes rubbing against interior walls or getting jammed in the doors. Leave another 60cm between the cupboard front and any other piece of furniture to allow the doors to open, or where space is tight, use sliding doors.

You need more drawers and shelves than hanging space. Have drawers of depths appropriate to the items being stored, and shelves for sweaters.

Many people prefer the romantic feel of a room furnished with freestanding furniture. A beautiful armoire, dressing table or chest of drawers will give a room a focal point. But bear in mind that a single, stand-alone wardrobe is rarely large enough to accommodate more than one person's clothes. Choose the largest piece a room can happily accommodate, or where the room is shared, invest in a pair of wardrobes.

ACCESSORIES

Accessories require specialised storage if they're not to clutter a space. Belts and ties should be hung or rolled, ideally in dedicated drawers. And if you don't want your shoes to occupy dimly lit spaces under the bed or in the wardrobe, they can be kept neatly on pull-out shelves or racks at the wardrobe's bottom, on sliding shelves or in organisers for hanging on the back of a door.

bedroom walls&floors

The bedroom is all about feeling good. It's spared most of the wear and tear of daily life, so you can be a little indulgent with what goes on the walls and floors, choosing finishes for how they look rather than for durability. When selecting surfaces for the bedroom, it's a case of if it feels good, go for it.

1. A subtly patterned carpet and a similarly restrained colour scheme on the walls make this a pleasant place to dream.
2. Touch-me textures define this handsome scheme, with khaki-coloured chenille on the walls and smooth parquetry underfoot.
3. The painted plasterboard walls and mixed hardwood floor in this room are easy to live with. A screen of Syrian cedar is suspended from the ceiling to bring a more intimate scale to the space.
4. A well-loved antique Portuguese gilt bed inspired an exotic setting, with gold-and-charcoal striped wallpaper and a soft blue carpet.
5. Walls upholstered in dark green cashmere suiting fabric create a quiet opulence. The light-coloured ceiling and pale sisal on the floor underscore the generous size of this bedroom.

WALLS

Paint, wallpaper, fabric… really there's little that doesn't work on a bedroom wall. The only proviso is that the surface must be easy to keep free of dust.

Paint is the most popular finish, but choose a low-fume formula for easy breathing. The bedroom is one room where the ceiling is observed as much as the walls, so you can make it a feature by picking out details in the cornice or painting it in a contrasting colour to the walls.

If walls are less than perfect, disguise their flaws with wallpaper, but be subtle when it comes to patterns. A visual collision between patterned walls and a busy-looking bedcover is far from restful. If walls are patterned, the rest of the furnishings should be plain, and vice versa.

Upholstering the walls is a more opulent treatment, but can attract dust. The fabric should be treated with a stain-resistant spray and regularly vacuumed.

Some newer apartments have one large space where a sliding screen can be pulled across to section off the sleeping and living zones when needed. In this case, walls should be finished in a neutral colour so the two areas work in harmony.

FLOORS

What you put on the floor in a bedroom must feel pleasant on your bare feet. Carpet is a favourite in this room as it's quiet, warm and soft to the touch. And as it's not subjected to as much foot traffic, it doesn't have to be purely practical. The bedroom is where shag-pile can rule.

Natural floorcoverings are also popular, though not everyone will like the roughness of coir. Flat-weave sisal has a super-smooth surface which feels almost like silk, and jute is also soft underfoot.

It's important that all soft floorcoverings are vacuumed regularly to keep them free of dust, otherwise you may find your snoozing turns into snuffling or wheezing.

Polished timber floors are another option. Warm and smooth underfoot and easy to clean, they are a real plus for people with allergies. The minus is that they can be a bit noisy and the surface finish will eventually wear. But if you put a rug next to the bed, you'll protect that section of floor which gets the most use.

Vinyl is good in kids' rooms, where you can expect frequent spills.

bedroom lighting&windows

Your sense of well-being is hugely dependent on the amount of light entering your home; rooms which attract minimal light or have been shut up for days have a negative, draining vibe. In a bedroom, it's a balancing trick getting the right levels of light. Lighting should be subdued, but bright enough for reading and not so strong it disturbs a sleeping partner. Bedside lamps and dimmers are essential here.

1

WINDOWS

Sunshine makes a bedroom look peaceful and warm. But while a steal of sunshine is delightful at 6.30am, it's less appealing at 5am. You must be able to dim the light so you can sleep past dawn or nap in the afternoon, yet allow in enough so you can see what you're doing.

Curtains, blinds and shutters are the easiest way to control how much light slips through the window. They also protect your privacy when you dress and while you are sleeping.

If you like waking in a sun-filled room, use sheer curtains, paper blinds, roller blinds or venetian blinds. These diffuse the sun's rays and give a cooler, more mellow atmosphere. But they won't have the same insulating effect as lined curtains, so expect brisk mornings in

winter. If you prefer a darker room, hang heavy lined curtains at the window. Timber shutters also block the light and have the advantage of allowing through breezes for ventilation.

While sheers are adequate for privacy during the day, when the bedroom lights are turned on, you'll need additional blinds or drapes if you want to avoid entertaining passers-by. A double curtain is a practical option: a sheer curtain lets through the light, while heavier drapes block out both sunlight and noise.

LIGHTING

Although the bedroom's main role is for sleeping, night lighting must be adequate. Reading in bed requires proper task lighting, and having the option to dim the main light will add to the restful mood.

1. A city apartment bedroom with glazing on two sides attracts plenty of sunshine. In summer, the windows are shielded with roller blinds in sunscreen fabric (woven PVC-coated fibreglass). In winter, the blinds are rolled up and the sun is welcomed in. **2.** Wide plantation shutters, made of stained timber, can be adjusted to let in more or less light to this bright, contemporary bedroom.

1. Metal louvres on the outside and roller blinds on the inside are a clever combination for controlling light, temperature and privacy.
2. With an all-glass wall on the rear of the house, this mezzanine bedroom had to be made less open. Fitting shutters above the balustrade retains the wash of sunlight and air, but means the occupants aren't putting on a show for the neighbours. Low-voltage halogen downlights create an even ambient light at night.
3. Simple sheer patterned curtains add inviting colour and diffuse the sunshine. The check fabric used on the padded headboard and valance gives a solid base to the floral fancy. Twin table lamps feature a classic style.
4. In this attic bedroom, privacy is protected by an opaque fabric screen which pulls up from the floor.
5. Windows extending to the floor allow in natural light and a view of the neighbourhood. But if privacy is required, a tug on the white roller blinds transforms the bedroom into a truly private space.

5

A PRACTICAL LIGHTING PLAN

The bedroom's main role is as somewhere to relax; it must be a place where it's easy to fall asleep and pleasant to wake. The ambient lighting should provide a neutral, calming background. You'll also need task lighting for reading.

● The bedroom should be soothing to the senses, so use softer lighting in rooms with strongly coloured walls. Remember that white walls will act as a reflector, so don't go overboard with high-wattage bulbs.

● A central pendant light is the usual in a bedroom, but it can make a room look dull and flat. Uplighters on the walls, which bounce light off the ceiling, will give a more subtle and interesting effect. You can also try adjustable spotlights to throw light off the walls, or concealed strip lighting around the edge of the room for a gentle, indirect light.

● It's annoying having to get out of bed to switch off the light, so fit on-off switches close by the bed as well as by the door.

● By installing a dimmer switch to the main light, you can adjust the brightness level to suit your mood.

● Adjustable table or wall-mounted lamps on each side of the bed are suitable for reading. If you and your bedmate read at different times, make sure each light has its own switch.

● Put lampshades on your bedside lights – they'll stop things being too glary on tired eyes. If they're table lamps, fit an opaque shade so the light is thrown downwards onto the book rather than onto the pillow. Needless to say, getting the lamp at the right height is critical – neither too high nor too low.

● If you have a dressing table or mirror, it should be properly lit. The light should be positioned so it shines on your face, rather than on the back of your head. Ceiling-mounted track lighting or a directional downlight both do the job.

● Interior lights in wardrobes are a practical idea. As well as making it easier to pick out clothes, it means you won't have to disturb your partner by switching on the main light if you get up earlier.

bedroom furniture

The main function of any bedroom is to provide a comfortable place to sleep. In fact, the bed is the most important piece of furniture in the house – it's where you slumber for eight hours each day, regathering your strength and sanity before venturing out into the busy world. The traditional bedroom suite includes a bed, bedside tables, a chest of drawers and a wardrobe, but today, anything goes. How you furnish your bedroom is really a matter of personal taste.

1. Large enough to be a private suite, this bedroom exhibits a light-hearted interpretation of classical style. Toile de Jouy fabric and pale gold and white highlights keep the mood light.
2. Bedside tables come in contemporary form, too. Here, a cantilevered unit means fewer legs for a more spacious effect.
3. A traditional armoire and bergere chair bring a French decorating style to the room. A chair is very useful in a bedroom as a place to read or just to tie shoelaces.

BEDS

Your bed defines the style of your bedroom. It's hardly a surprise, as it's the biggest, most obvious piece of furniture in the room. Four-posters, Victorian-style cast-iron beds and sleigh beds bring a sense of romance, while sleek timber platform beds are leaders of the mod squad. But even a demure style of bed can become eye-catching if you put on a colourful quilt or add a headboard.

Remember, a bed base on castors is easier to move and make. And if you love watching television or reading in bed, an adjustable bed base that can move into different lying and seating positions could be your idea of heaven.

A headboard provides support when you're sitting up. Padded headboards are the most comfortable, but you should be able to remove the cover for washing, so it doesn't start looking the worse for wear.

You spend more hours sleeping on a bed than you do driving a car, so buy the best you can afford. The bed base and the mattress should be suited to each other, as it's the two combined that will give you a good night's sleep.

Don't be tempted to put a new mattress on a worn-out base. The mattress will end up lumpy and uncomfortable, and last only about a third as long.

Bed bases can be timber-slatted or solid timber, wire mesh attached to an outer wooden frame, a box-spring (the bottom part of an inner-spring mattress ensemble), or a water bed.

Box-spring mattresses work like shock absorbers and extend the life of a mattress, although they're not as well ventilated as timber-slatted or wire-mesh bases. More expensive box-spring bases are sprung-edge, with springs mounted on top of the wooden frame so there's a similar amount of support all over. Firm-edge bases are cheaper and, as the name suggests, have no springs on top of the frame, so are harder around the edges.

MATTRESSES

There are several styles of mattress, but whatever you choose, it must keep your spine straight while you sleep. A mattress that's too soft or hard can cause your spine to kink, leading to back problems.

Inner-spring mattresses These have a series of wire coils with layers of padding on top. Pillowtop mattresses have a quilted treatment on top of the padding. Some inner-springs are made for a box-spring base, and you should buy the whole ensemble at the same time; others suit timber or wire-mesh bases. The more coils in the mattress, the firmer the support.
Lifespan At least 10 years if the mattress is vacuumed and turned regularly.
Latex mattresses Made from aerated natural rubber, latex mattresses offer excellent back support, are very durable and don't harbour dust mites, making them good for people with allergies and asthma. They're at the luxury end of the market.
Lifespan Up to 15 years.

1. A romantic look doesn't always mean ruffles and chintz. This four-poster bed is made dreamy with a sheer canopy and pastel-patterned bedlinen.
2. This upholstered bed base and ottoman create a streamlined look, as there are no fussy overhangs from a bedspread.
3. A hanging tapestry gives this sleigh bed more presence. The tapestry is an alternative to a headboard, and draws the bed and side tables into one visual unit. Two armchairs cosy up by the window to invite conversation.

BUYING A MATTRESS
- Always try before you buy. Lie on a mattress in your normal sleeping position for 15 to 30 minutes before making a decision.
- Your mattress should be 15cm longer than the tallest sleeper and wide enough so you can lie back and bend your elbows without touching your partner or hanging over the edge of the bed.
- A mattress should be firm enough to keep your spine straight while you sleep. Lie face-up on the bed and slip your hand underneath the small of your back. If your hand slides under easily, the bed is too hard. If you can't get your hand under at all, it's too soft.

NUMBERS TO KNOW
- Standard bed sizes are: single, 92cm wide by 188cm long; double, 137cm wide by 188cm long; queen 153cm wide by 203cm long; and king, 183cm wide by 203cm long.
- Allow a corridor of space 75cm wide around a bed (except where it's pushed up against the wall), or 95cm if doors open into that area.
- Allow 60-75cm of space in front of wardrobe doors.
- A chest of drawers needs 95cm of space in front, and a dressing table requires 60cm so a chair can be pulled in and out easily.

Foam mattresses These are easy on the budget and don't attract dust mites, so suit people with allergies. But buy one made of good quality foam or the mattress will start sagging in no time.
Lifespan Expect two years for medium-density foam; up to 10 years for extra-high-density foam.
Futons Inexpensive, Japanese-style futons are made of layers of cotton, wool or polyester, although some have a foam core or a centre of rubberised coir. Futons are very comfortable, but require a little care. Damp destroys them, making the wadding lose its bounce and encouraging mould. To combat this, futons should be aired and left in the sun regularly.
Lifespan If looked after, traditional or foam-core futons last three to five years; coir-centre futons last five to seven years.
Water beds These consist of a water bladder and heater (to warm the water) held in a frame. They distribute body weight evenly, with no pressure points, and are good for allergy sufferers. Newer, soft-sided water beds hold a water bladder in a foam block and have a zip-on cover, so they look like an inner-spring ensemble.
Lifespan They should last at least 10 years. Replacement water bladders and soft-side foam blocks are available.

OTHER FURNITURE
Bedside tables are often coordinated with the headboard, and sometimes are part of the headboard. If the bedside table is to be a base for a reading lamp, power points should be located close by. Height is important: if the table's too low, the lamp won't be high enough to throw out a usable light; if it's too high, you'll have to sit up to reach things.

A small chair can be handy to drape clothes over, while an armchair, ottoman or window seat offers a private space for reading or putting on your shoes.

Good storage is essential in the bedroom if you haven't a designated walk-in dressing room. Traditional chests of drawers, wardrobes and shelving all help keep clutter under control, but increasingly their role is being taken over by built-in storage systems.

Built-ins are a boon in small bedrooms, as an entire wall has the potential to be turned into storage. But they lack the character and versatility of freestanding furniture, which can be moved around the room whenever you want.

Remember, uniformity isn't essential: choosing pieces of a similar era, or having an eclectic mix united by similar colours, will give an interesting look.

A separate playroom, with plenty of clear floor space and built-in storage, takes the action away from the quieter sleeping zones. It can be given immense character with fabric and paint. This play space is adjacent to Riley and Alex's attic bedrooms.

children

In a real family home with real kids, no room is sacred. It's a myth that you can contain them and their gear and continue life as carefree grown-ups. It simply will not happen. The trade-off, however, is that a home without them would be less vibrant. It would lack the spontaneity and excitement that their energy brings to a space. Of course, children should have their special kids' zone; an area that's tuned into their activities, interests and passions. It's a place where you can be clever with furniture and storage options, and be playful with colour schemes for tots to teens. But don't forget about safety — it's incredibly important when you're designing for kids.

childrenzones

Children bring living colour to a home. They encourage communication and creativity, and a home seems to radiate with the joy, not to mention the noise, of their presence. But children definitely alter the way you think and the way you approach decorating your home. They make demands on space, furniture and your time, and you must be efficient and inventive in adapting your house to cope.

1. PLAY

Children of all ages gravitate to the floor, whether they're piecing together a jigsaw puzzle or playing on their Game Boy™. It makes sense to have a clean sweep of floor for them to spread out comfortably. Just make sure the area is out of the way of cross traffic. This high-energy scheme with floor-hugging furniture is ideal for a teenager. The multi-purpose table has drawers to keep CDs and magazines tidy.

2. READING

When a child begins pre-school it is time to add table and chairs to their room, to encourage them to sit (still) and look at their picture books. A corner of the room should be kept clear for this activity. As a child becomes an independent reader, of course, this table will be replaced with a desk and well-designed ergonomic chair. This hand-painted solid wood table setting is the perfect size for pre-schoolers.

3. HOMEWORK/STUDY

Primary school comes with a new set of activities: friends to play with, sleep-overs and, of course, homework. While it's not the optimum to have a computer in the bedroom, many kids use one for entertainment as well as schoolwork. Old school desks make great computer tables, but a desk that's part of a platform bed system is useful when space is tight.

4. PERSONAL SPACE

The bed is the centrepiece of children's rooms and they must love it unconditionally. Be sure it's positioned where they feel comfortable. Ask them; they'll tell you where. Good design and children can co-exist and this beautiful custom-made limewashed bed is just what little Portia likes playing on.

5. NURSERY NECESSITIES

It's important you have a well-ventilated, light-filled zone dedicated to the mechanics of baby life. A change table should be easily accessible, with good storage. In this attic nursery, a trestle table makes the perfect change table and later it can be used as a desk. There's also a comfortable, slip-covered chair for nursing.

THINK OF THE FUTURE

Territorial areas for children are generally the bedroom, playroom and family room and all should feel welcoming and safe. Whether you're preparing for the arrival of a new baby or renovating because the children have outgrown their old bedrooms, do your homework first in terms of planning. Establish some priorities. Will the rooms be shared? And will the rooms be used progressively by more than one child? Will the bedroom double as a play area? Is the room suitable to adapt to more furniture in the years to come? Can extra storage be added later? Is the flooring hard-wearing and able to cope with mess, yet be kind to little feet? Let's be honest here – many children's rooms are created by parents for parents. It's the grown-ups who find the paraphernalia associated with children (and babies) too exciting to resist. Indeed for first-time parents it's all part of the fun of their new role in life.

A general rule with designing for children is to avoid the permanent fixtures and fittings of childhood; they can be rapidly outgrown and become redundant. For example, built-in, small-scale furniture and painted fairytale motifs will inevitably become hugely uncool in pre-teen years.

Keeping the decoration simple and selecting furniture with easy-care surfaces is a practical approach for children's bedrooms. After the baby and toddler stages, your children will decorate the space themselves with their toys, photographs, posters, artworks and general clutter.

It's a good idea to get the basics right from the beginning. Keep an eye to the years ahead, and carry out any structural alterations like replacing windows, putting in extra power points (the computer, DVD player, television and mobile phone charger are mandatory in teen years) and installing heating, or even an ensuite.

childrencolour&decoration

Go for the three Cs… colour, comfort and creativity when planning an environment for children. And go easy on the cutesy decorative themes and focus on what kids really want in their rooms. Credit them with good taste and involve them in the planning of the colour scheme. But hold fire on the decoration when they are young, because children always want what is too old for them. Posters of their sports heroes might be cool, but for a youngster eager to grow up, black walls and heavy metal posters can wait.

1. RELATED COLOURS

This scheme uses colours or shades of colours that lie close to each on the colour wheel (see page 24). The effect is calming and harmonious. In this toddler's bedroom, the colours are introduced in themed fabric that has been made up into simple, elegant drapes and a pelmet.

2. COMPLEMENTARY WITH TERTIARY COLOURS

Incorporating colours that sit opposite each other on the colour wheel produces a buzz (see page 24). Tones of red and blue, two of the primary colours, really hit it off and make a great combination in this room belonging to a young, active boy who likes fishing and outdoor sports.

3. COMPLEMENTARY WITH SECONDARY COLOURS

This scheme balances warm and cool colours of red and green, and those intermediate colours which fall between primary and secondary colours on the colour wheel (see page 24). Red is an advancing colour, so the check fabric on the bed and wardrobe has loads of impact. The combination is sophisticated enough for a young adult.

4. MONOCHROMATIC

Yellow is used in varying strengths and tones to emphasise the whimsical check pattern in Siena's room. A subtle windowpane check is painted on the walls and cotton gingham features in the soft furnishings.

childrencolour&decoration

1

BABY BOOM

Spending buckets of money on a
'baby' scheme is wasteful. Instead,
choose a colour combination (like
blue and yellow or creamy white)
that will last through childhood.
Babies and toddlers spend most
of their day on the floor, so fix a
wallpaper border at skirting level.
Include a block-out roller blind on
the window to encourage naps.

PRIMARY HIGHLIGHTS

School-age kids often want their
rooms themed around favourite
characters. Wallpaper borders are
the cheapest way to theme a room,
and can be removed easily when
the child tires of them; novelty
bedlinen is another easy option.
Hobbies are big at this age, so have
pinboards and shelves where your
kids can show off their efforts.

TIPS FOR TEENS

Abandon any notion of having
much say in the style of a teenager's
room. Remember that selecting a
colour means selecting an identity.
But if he or she wants a vibrantly
coloured room, make sure there is
a more muted study zone and
sleeping area. Computers, stereos,
posters and even backpacks will add
plenty of colour to this private world.

COLOUR SENSE

Children are born into a world of colour
extravagance. They can have anything
and everything in colour, from plastic
toys to computers and stereos. Just like
adults, kids prefer some hues over others.
If you don't already know what colours
your offspring prefer, toss a packet of coloured pencils on a table and watch as they
pick their favourites and begin to draw.

Today's cyber kids adore colour. But
because they expect… no, demand change,
they choose colours they relate to at the
time. Not all parents will be prepared
to indulge a child's every colour whim.
Let's face it, wall-to-wall purple, black or
brown would overwhelm most of us, no
matter how cool our kids tell us it is.

Try to avoid typecasting. Give your
child a canvas onto which they can
stamp their personality with their favourite things – particularly boys, who can be
more inhibited when it comes to colour.

The scheme should be conducive to
both sleep and activity. For instance,
while the hot, intense colours of red,
yellow and orange are claimed to acceler-
ate activity and stimulate the brain, they
could also prevent a child sleeping well.

You may want to take the middle
ground by opting for softer shades of
those colours, like pink, buttermilk and
pale terracotta. However, if your child
is passionate about bright colour, com-
promise by painting the room in neutral
tones and using the hot colour for the
door or a feature wall.

Remember, whatever colour your child
selects, there is a spectrum of decorating
solutions to complement it.

children furniture&storage

Bedrooms are special places for children; they are somewhere to call their own, where they can store (and hide!) personal treasures and where they can create and become lost in their own fantasy worlds. But let's be realistic; lost is the operative word here. Unless storage needs are accounted for early in a child's life, there will never be any law and order to the room and the frenetic search for misplaced possessions will eventually drive a parent mad. Bedroom furniture, like storage, requires careful attention to detail, so plan your child's room according to their activities and be prepared for a challenge.

1. These wardrobes have been painted with storybook houses.
2. Office trays keep accessories in order under the bed.
3. A tubular-steel frame bed is popular for school-age kids. Let the bedlinen inspire a decorative theme.
4. Earmark a corner for treasures. Make it special with a drop of wallpaper and timber shelves.
5. A table can hold anything from bedside books to a CD player. A pinboard above displays cards and certificates.
6. A tiny tower of drawers is for precious items.
7. In a baby's room, pigeonholes and labelled baskets store folded clothes and toys.
8. Storage around a window tidies children's knick-knacks. The wicker baskets hold toys.

FOR SAFETY'S SAKE

● Paint on walls and furniture must be lead-free (water-based is best) and other surfaces must be non-toxic.
● Avoid sharp and splintery edges on furnishings, and constantly review the toy collection.
● Freestanding bookcases and dressers should be screwed to walls.
● Don't put a chair or bed under a window in a baby or toddler's room, as it can entice them to climb out.
● Fit windows with safety catches.
● Fit safety covers on power points.
● Use wall-mounted lamps.
● Be sure a baby's cot complies with national safety standards.
● Bunk beds must have a safety rail and a secured ladder. You can also fit a safety rail to a small child's bed.

STOW AND SNOOZE

● Children's rooms demand good storage, but at first you'll only need drawers for folded baby clothes and nappy gear.
● When children start wanting to choose their outfits for themselves, add a wardrobe system with a hanging section.
● At school age, kids need a 'big bed', chair and desk for homework. They also need a place for books and plenty of deep drawers for toys. Little boxes keep stickers, jewellery and so on organised.

● Big boxes and plastic crates can store oddly shaped items. Pigeonhole shelving can take crates or storage baskets.
● Don't make shelving too lightweight as some children tend to pull it over.
● Children love beds in fantasy shapes: little girls adore four-posters and boys like bunk beds and divans. But choose a mattress that supports their growing bodies.
● Teenagers require more of a bed-sitting room. Floor cushions and divan beds that don't look like beds will suit the mood.

2

3

4

5

6

7

8

acknowledgments

P: Photography
A: Architecture
ID: Interior design
D: Design

FRONT COVER P: Simon Kenny.
Pg 2 P: Dan Magree.
Pg 5 P: Dan Magree.
LIVING
Pg 8 P: Alan Benson.
LIVING ZONES
Pg 10 1. **P:** Simon Kenny. **D:** Terril Riley-Gibson, Rozelle, NSW. 2. **P:** Dan Magree. **D:** Hecker Phelan, St Kilda, Vic. 3. **P:** Eric Victor-Perdraut. **D:** Anne Enright Burns, Brisbane, Qld.
Pg 11 4. **P:** Dean Wilmot. **D:** Bucich Studios, Double Bay, NSW.
Pg 12 5. **P:** Simon Kenny. **D:** James Durie, Patio, Surry Hills, NSW.
Pg 13 6. **P:** Dan Magree. **D:** Katy Richardson, Melbourne, Vic. 7. **P:** Oliver Ford, Photographix. 8. **P:** Gaelle Le Boulicaut. **A:** James Grose, Grose Bradley Architects, Sydney, NSW. 9. **P:** Dan Magree. Artwork: "Loose Leaves" by Jo Sabey, St Kilda, Vic.
LIVING STYLE
Pg 14 1. **P:** Andre Martin. Shot at Dockside King Street Wharf, Sydney, NSW. **A:** Cox Richardson/Crone Associates, Sydney, NSW. **ID:** Idiom Design Practice, Surry Hills, NSW.
Pg 15 2. **P:** Dan Magree. **D:** Lou Lockwood, Toorak, Vic.
Pg 16 3. **P:** Eric Victor-Perdraut. **ID:** John England, Brisbane, Qld.
Pg 17 4. **P:** Simon Kenny. **ID:** Peter Reeve, CRD, Darlinghurst, NSW: 5. **P:** Simon Kenny. **A:** HPA Architects, North Sydney, NSW. **ID:** Michael Jones and Tom Chin, Sydney, NSW.
Pg 18 6. **P:** Eric Victor-Perdraut. **A:** Gabriel and Elizabeth Poole for Lensworth Kawana Waters, Caloundra, Qld. 7. **P:** Simon Kenny. **D:** KGD, Glebe, NSW.
Pg 19 8. **P:** Dan Magree. **D:** David Hicks, Prahran, Vic.
Pg 20 9. **P:** Alice Pagliano. Artwork: Photographs on wall by Anna and Bernhard Blume.
Pg 21 10. **P:** Rodney Weidland. 11. **P:** Simon Kenny. **A:** Peter Lonergan, Cracknell & Lonergan, Camperdown, NSW. Artwork: Painting by Fabia Tory.
LIVING COLOUR
Pg 22 1. **P:** Andre Martin. Shot at Dockside King Street Wharf, Sydney, NSW. Architect: Cox Richardson/Crone Associates, Sydney, NSW. **ID:** Idiom Design Practice & Cox Interiors, Surry Hills, NSW. 2. **P:** Jeff Kilpatrick. **A:** Luke Middleton, Brearley Middleton, South Yarra, Vic. Artwork: Painting by Jenny Watson. 3. **P:** Bill Anagrius. **A:** Nick Rickard, Drummoyne, NSW.
Pg 23 4. **P:** Simon Kenny. **D:** Architect Peter Lonergan, Cracknell & Lonergan, Camperdown, NSW. 5. **P:** David Morcombe. **A:** Simon Rodrigues, Odden Rodrigues Architects, Claremont, WA. 6. **P:** Dan Magree. **A:** Irena Lobaza, Hugh Basset & Irena Lobaza Architects, Yarraville, Vic. **ID:** Fiona Austin, Stonehenge Interior Design, South Melbourne, Vic.
Pg 24 1. **P:** Maree Homer. 2. **P:** Andre Martin.
Pg 25 P: Gaelle Le Boulicaut. Artwork: Paintings by Naomi Simson.
LIVING STORAGE
Pg 26 1. **P:** Mark Green.
Pg 27 2. **P:** Simon Griffiths. **A:** Neometro, St Kilda, Vic. **ID:** Hermon & Hermon Plus, Richmond, Vic.
Pg 28 1. **P:** Dan Magree. **A:** Peter Maddison and Antony Di Mase, Maddison Architects, South Melbourne, Vic. 2. **P:** Simon Kenny. **ID:** Alexandra McKenzie, Alexandra McKenzie Interiors, Elizabeth Bay, NSW. 3. **P:** Simon Kenny. **ID:** Shellee Gordoun, Interiors with Zest, Moore Park, NSW. 4. **P:** Simon Kenny. **A:** Peter Lonergan, Cracknell & Lonergan, Camperdown, NSW. 5. **P:** Simon Kenny. 6. **P:** Dan Magree. 7. **P:** Simon Griffiths. **A:** Nic Bochsler, Bochsler & Partners, Toorak, Vic. 8. **P:** Dan Magree. 9. **P:** Simon Kenny.
Pg 29 10. **P:** Simon Kenny.
LIVING WALLS & FLOORS
Pg 30 1. **P:** Eric Victor-Perdraut. Artwork: From Fire-Works Gallery, Fortitude Valley, Qld. 2. **P:** Dan Magree. 3 **P:** Simon Kenny. **ID:** Concepts Interior Design, Deakin, ACT. Artwork: Charcoal by Dana Tosolini.
Pg 31 4. **P:** Dan Magree.
Pg 32 1. **P:** Simon Kenny. **A:** Brian Meyerson, Bondi, NSW. **ID:** Shellee Gordoun, Interiors With Zest, Moore Park, NSW.
Pg 33 2. **P:** Andre Martin. **A:** Adam Pearson Design and Adam Pearson/ Joanne Case Architects, Paddington, NSW.
LIVING LIGHTING & WINDOWS
Pg 34 1. **P:** Simon Kenny. **A:** Misho Vasiljevich, Misho & Associates, East Sydney, NSW. 2. **P:** Simon Kenny. **D:** Iain Halliday, Burley Katon Halliday, Paddington, NSW. 3. **P:** Courtesy Designers Guild, London, UK. Fabrics from Designers Guild Zandanechi collection.
Pg 35 4. **P:** Andrew Elton. **A:** Richard Neath, Group GSA, East Sydney, NSW. Artwork: "Mateus" rose painting by Gwyneth Stephens.
Pg 37 1. **P:** Simon Griffiths. **ID:** Agatha Lim, Inter.Scape Design, South Yarra, Vic. 2. **P:** Andrew Lehmann. **A:** Renzo Piano, Genoa, Italy. 3. **P:** Simon Kenny. 4. **P:** Simon Kenny. **A:** HPM Architects, North Sydney, NSW. **ID:** Michael Jones and Tom Chin, Sydney, NSW.
LIVING FURNITURE
Pg 38 1. **P:** Dan Magree. Artwork: By Jules Sher, from Australian Art Resources. 2. **P:** Simon Kenny. **ID:** Ruth Levine, Ruth Levine Designs, Paddington, NSW. 3. **P:** Simon Kenny. **A:** Alexander Tzannes, Chippendale, NSW. **ID:** Scott Weston Architect & Design, East Sydney, NSW.
Pg 39 4. **P:** Andre Martin. Artwork: By Gordon Richards.
Pg 40 1. **P:** Dan Magree. **ID:** Lou Lockwood, Toorak, Vic. 2. **P:** Simon Kenny. **A:** Misho Vasiljevich, Misho & Associates, East Sydney, NSW. 3. **P:** Dan Magree. **A:** Bruce Allen, Bruce Allen & John Courmadias Pty Ltd, Melbourne, Vic. **ID:** Fiona Austin, Stonehenge Interior Design, Richmond, Vic. 4. **P:** Bill Anagrius. **ID:** Sandra Zobel, Zobel Interiors, Balmoral, NSW.
Pg 41 5. **P:** Dan Magree. **ID:** Richard Waples, Guilford Bell & Graham Fisher Architects, South Yarra, Vic.
Pg 42 1. **P:** Warwick Kent. **ID:** Alma Maccallum and Jeff Paterson, Cremorne Point, NSW. Artwork: Painting by Max Mansell. 2. **P:** Trevor Fox.
Pg 43 3. **P:** Eric Victor-Perdraut. **A:** Penny Campbell and Ed Haysom, Haysom Spender Architects, Brisbane, Qld. Artwork: Glass art by Gary Nash.
LIVING ARRANGEMENT & DETAIL
Pg 44 1. **P:** Dan Magree. Artwork: Painting by Robyn Rankin.
Pg 45 2. **P:** Simon Kenny.
Pg 46 1. **P:** Simon Kenny. 2. **P:** Andre Martin. 3. **P:** Simon Kenny. **ID:** Sarah Davidson, Sydney, NSW. 4. **P:** Simon Kenny. **ID:** Alexandra McKenzie Interiors, Elizabeth Bay, NSW. 5. **P:** Jeff Kilpatrick. **ID:** Charlotte Heine, Albert Park, Vic. 6. **P:** Dan Magree. 7. **P:** Simon Kenny. 8. **P:** Dan Magree. 9. **P:** Dan Magree.
Pg 47 10. **P:** Simon Kenny. **ID:** Linda Kerry, Double Bay, NSW.
Pg 48 1. **P:** Simon Kenny. 2. **P:** Gaelle Le Boulicaut.
Pg 49 3. **P:** Dan Magree. 4. **P:** Simon Kenny. **ID:** Leroy Belle, Darlinghurst, NSW. 5. **P:** Dan Magree. Artwork: Painting by Rachel Perkin. 6. **P:** Bill Anagrius.
KITCHEN
Pg 50 P: Mark Green. **D:** Linda James, Pymble, NSW.
KITCHEN ZONES
Pg 52 1. **P:** Dan Magree. **A:** Irena Lobaza, Hugh Basset & Irena Lobaza Architects, Yarraville, Vic. **ID:** Fiona Austin, Stonehenge Interior Design, South Melbourne, Vic. 2. **P:** Rodney Weidland. **ID:** Maxwell J Interiors, St Peters, NSW. 3. **P:** Greg McBean.
Pg 53 4. **P:** Simon Kenny.
Pg 54 5. **P:** Simon Kenny. **ID:** Hare + Klein, Woolloomooloo, NSW.
Pg 55 6. **P:** Dan Magree. **A:** Col Bandy Architect, Windsor, Vic. 7. **P:** Chris Bennett. **ID:** Melinda Boag Design, Yarralumla, ACT. 8. **P:** Simon Kenny. **A:** Leo Campbell, Campbell Luscombe Associates, Waterloo, NSW. 9. **P:** Simon Kenny. **A:** Peter Lonergan, Cracknell & Lonergan, Camperdown, NSW.
KITCHEN LAYOUT
Pg 56 1. **P:** Simon Kenny. **ID:** Meryl Hare, Hare + Klein, Woolloomooloo, NSW. 2. **P:** Simon Kenny. **A:** Kim Crestani, Order Architects, Hunters Hill, NSW. 3. **P:** David Morcombe. **A:** Debra Brown, Hofman & Brown, Cottesloe, WA.
Pg 57 4. **P:** Dan Magree. 5. **P:** Simon Griffiths. **ID:** Christopher Connell Design, Melbourne, Vic. 6. **P:** Andrew Elton. **A:** Richard Neath, Group GSA, East Sydney, NSW.
KITCHEN STYLE
Pg 58 1. **P:** Simon Kenny. **A:** Brian Meyerson, Bondi, NSW. **ID:** Shellee Gordoun, Interiors with Zest, Moore Park, NSW.
Pg 59 2. **P:** Neil Lorimer.
Pg 60 3. **P:** Bill Anagrius. **A:** Philip Diement, Surry Hills, NSW. **ID:** David Walton, Darlinghurst, NSW.
Pg 61 4. **P:** Eric Victor-Perdraut. **A:** Paul Uhlmann, Burleigh Heads, Qld.
Pg 62 5. **P:** David Morcombe. 6. **P:** David Morcombe. **A:** Simon Rodrigues, Odden Rodrigues Architects, Claremont, WA.
Pg 63 7. **P:** Neil Lorimer. **ID:** Geoffrey Brown & Associates, Hawthorn, Vic.
Pg 64 8. **P:** Andre Martin. **D:** Bush Country Homes, Eglinton, NSW.
Pg 65 9. **P:** Chris Bennett. **ID:** Melinda Boag Design, Yarralumla, ACT. 10. **P:** Nigel Noyes.
KITCHEN COLOUR
Pg 66 1. **P:** Eric Victor-Perdraut. **ID:** black + spiro, New Farm, Qld. 2. **P:** Bill Anagrius. **ID:** Nerida Nicholas, Sydney, NSW. 3. **P:** Alan Benson. **ID:** Concepts Interior Design, Deakin, ACT.
Pg 67 4. **P:** Hamilton Lund. **ID:** Heather Buttrose Associates, Woolloomooloo, NSW. 5. **P:** Eric Victor-Perdraut. **A:** Paul Uhlmann, Burleigh Heads, Qld. 6. **P:** Jeff Kilpatrick. **A:** Bruce Katsipidis, Aktis, North Fitzroy, Vic.
Pg 68 1. **P:** Andre Martin. 2. **P:** Valerie Martin. 3. **P:** Dan Magree. 4. **P:** Simon Kenny. 5. **P:** Dan Magree. 6. **P:** Simon Kenny. 7. **P:** Simon Kenny. 8. **P:** Andre Martin.
Pg 69 9. **P:** Simon Griffiths. **ID:** Agatha Lim, Inter.Scape Design, South Yarra, Vic.
KITCHEN STORAGE
Pg 70 1. **P:** Simon Kenny.
Pg 71 2. **P:** Dan Magree. **A:** Irena Lobaza, Hugh Basset & Irena Lobaza Architects, Yarraville, Vic. **ID:** Fiona Austin, Stonehenge Interior Design, South Melbourne, Vic. 3. **P:** David Morcombe. **A:** Raymond Jones, North Fremantle, WA. **ID:** Armstrong Interiors, Mt Hawthorn, WA. 4. **P:** Eric Victor-Perdraut. **A:** Penny Campbell and Ed Haysom, Haysom Spender Architects, Brisbane, Qld. 5. **P:** Andre Martin. **A:** Michael Folk, Folk Lichtman & Associates, Waterloo, NSW. 6. **P:** Dan Magree.
Pg 72 1. **P:** Simon Kenny. **A:** Nick Cooney, Sydney, NSW. 2. **P:** Jeff Kilpatrick. **D:** Charlotte Heine, Albert Park, Vic. 3. **P:** Robert Frith. 4. **P:** Oliver Ford. **A:** Andrew Macens, Macens Associates, Epping, Vic. 5. **P:** Greg McBean. **ID:** Melinda Boag Design, Yarralumla, ACT. 6. **P:** Andre Martin. **A:** Leo Campbell, Campbell Luscombe Associates, Waterloo, NSW. 7. **P:** Eric Victor-Perdraut. 8. **P:** Jeff Kilpatrick. **D:** Charlotte Heine, Albert Park, Vic. 9. **P:** Neil Lorimer.
Pg 73 10. **P:** Bill Anagrius.
KITCHEN WALLS & FLOORS
Pg 74 1. **P:** Simon Kenny.
Pg 75 2. **P:** Rodney Hyett. **A:** Sean Godsell, Godsell Associates, South Yarra, Vic. 3. **P:** Dan Magree. **A:** John Wardle, John Wardle Architects, Melbourne, Vic.
Pg 76 1. **P:** Greg McBean. **ID:** Melinda Boag Design, Yarralumla, ACT. 2. **P:** Ray Main/Mainstream. Inlaid floor designed by William Yeoward, London, UK. 3. **P:** Dean Wilmot. **A:** Folk Lichtman & Associates, Waterloo, NSW. 4. **P:** Robert Frith. **A:** Philip McAllister Architects, Perth, WA.
KITCHEN LIGHTING & WINDOWS
Pg 78 1. **P:** Bill Anagrius. **A:** Platino Properties, Sydney, NSW. 2. **P:** Simon Kenny. **A:** Michael Folk, Folk Lichtman & Associates, Waterloo, NSW.
Pg 79 3. **P:** Mark Green. **D:** Linda James, Pymble, NSW.
Pg 80 1. **P:** Andrew Lehmann. **ID:** Greg Natale Interior Design, Surry Hills, NSW. 2. **P:** Mark Green. **A:** Caroline Pidcock Architects, East Sydney, NSW. 3. **P:** Eric Victor-Perdraut. **A:** Will Franklin, Noosaville, Qld. 4. **P:** Dan Magree. **ID:** Fiona Austin, Stonehenge Interior Design, South Melbourne, Vic.
Pg 81 5. **P:** Bill Anagrius. **D:** KJC Constructions, Mosman, NSW. 6. **P:** David Morcombe. **ID:** Jane Agnew, Mt Claremont, WA.
Pg 82 1. **P:** Rodney Weidland.
Pg 83 2. **P:** Eric Victor-Perdraut. **A:** Penny Campbell and Ed Haysom, Haysom Spender Architects, Brisbane, Qld.
KITCHEN BENCHTOPS & SPLASHBACKS
Pg 85 1. **P:** Jeff Kilpatrick. **A:** Bruce Katsipidis, Aktis, North Fitzroy, Vic. 2. **P:** Simon Kenny. **D:** Judy Williams, Balmain, NSW. 3. **P:** Simon Kenny. **ID:** Concepts Interior Design, Deakin, ACT. 4. **P:** Simon Kenny. Architect, Brian Meyerson, Bondi Junction, NSW.
Pg 86 1. **P:** Dan Magree. **A:** Steven Whiting, Whiting A+I, Albert Park, Vic. 2. **P:** David Morcombe. **A:** Simon Rodrigues, Odden Rodrigues Architects, Claremont, WA. 3. **P:** Chris Bennett. **D:** Artline Kitchens, Canberra, ACT. 4. **P:** Rodney Hyett. **A:** John Matyas Architects, Middle Park, Vic. 5. **P:** David Young. 6. **P:** David Morcombe. 7. **P:** David Morcombe. **A:** Tim Wright, Peppermint Grove, WA. 8. **P:** Dan Magree. **A:** Vincent Interlandi, Interlandi Design Group, Kew, Vic. 9. **P:** Neil Lorimer.
KITCHEN APPLIANCES
Pg 89 1. **P:** David Morcombe. **A:** Odden Rodrigues Architects, Claremont, WA.

2. **P:** Eric Victor-Perdraut. **ID:** Anna Spiro, black + spiro, New Farm, Qld. 3. **P:** Simon Kenny. 4. **P:** Andrew Lehmann. **ID:** Greg Natale Interior Design, Surry Hills, NSW.

Pg 90 1. **P:** David Morcombe. **A:** Richard Szklarz, Cottesloe, WA. 2. **P:** Alan Benson. **ID:** Concepts Interior Design, Deakin, ACT. 3. **P:** Dan Magree.

KITCHEN FURNITURE

Pg 92 1. **P:** Dan Magree.

Pg 93 2. **P:** Bill Anagrius. **A:** Nicholas Solomon, Larcombe & Solomon Architects, Surry Hills, NSW.

Pg 94 1. **P:** Dan Magree. **A:** Lyons, Melbourne, Vic. 2. **P:** Simon Kenny. **A:** Urban Moo, Surry Hills, NSW.

Pg 95 3. **P:** Eric Victor-Perdraut. **A:** Paul Owen Architects, Ascot, Qld. Artwork: By Rod Bunter.

KITCHEN LAUNDRY

Pg 96 1. **P:** Robert Frith. **A:** Richard Szklarz, Richard Szklarz Architects, Cottesloe, WA. 2. **P:** Robert Frith. **A:** Richard Szklarz Architects, Cottesloe, WA.

Pg 97 3. **P:** Simon Kenny. **A:** Bruce Townsend, Townsend & Associates Architects, O'Connor, ACT. 4. **P:** Dan Magree. **D:** Owner and David Mulhall, Accent On Design, Malvern, Vic. 5. **P:** Simon Kenny. **A:** Bruce Townsend, Townsend & Associates Architects, O'Connor, ACT. 6. **P:** Simon Kenny.

WORKING

Pg 98 **P:** Dan Magree. **A:** Irena Lobaza, Hugh Basset & Irena Lobaza Architects, Yarraville, Vic. **ID:** Fiona Austin, Stonehenge Interior Design, South Melbourne, Vic.

WORKING ZONES

Pg 100 1. **P:** Brett Boardman. **A:** Keith Pike, Sydney, NSW.

Pg 101 2. **P:** Jeff Kilpatrick. 3.&4. **P:** Dan Magree. **ID:** Elissa King, Sanders & King, Armadale, Vic. 5. **P:** Valerie Martin. **A:** Caroline Pidcock, East Sydney, NSW.

WORKING STYLE

Pg 102 1. **P:** Chris Bennett. **A:** Robert Peck von Hartel Trethowan Architects, Sydney, NSW.

Pg 103 2. **P:** Simon Kenny. Artwork: On desk, "Creation" by Carmen Soraya Moreno. 3. **P:** Simon Kenny. 4. **P:** Dan Magree. 5. **P:** Simon Kenny. **A:** Luke Cummins, Urban Moo, Surry Hills, NSW.

WORKING COLOUR

Pg 104 1. **P:** Simon Kenny. 2. **P:** Dan Magree.

Pg 105 3. **P:** Simon Kenny. **ID:** Villa Interiors, Crows Nest, NSW. 4. **P:** Jeff Kilpatrick. 5. **P:** Simon Kenny.

WORKING STORAGE & EQUIPMENT

Pg 106 1. **P:** Valerie Martin. **A:** Caroline Pidcock, East Sydney, NSW. 2. **P:** Simon Kenny. **A:** Luke Cummins, Urban Moo, Surry Hills, NSW. 3. **P:** Jeff Kilpatrick. 4. **P:** Eric Victor-Perdraut.

WORKING SURFACES & LIGHTING

Pg 108 1. **P:** Dan Magree. **A:** Irena Lobaza, Hugh Bassett & Irena Lobaza Architects, Yarraville, Vic.

Pg 109 2. **P:** Chris Bennett. **ID:** Bridget Tyer, North Sydney, NSW. 3. **P:** Trevor Fox. **A:** Phil Harris, Troppo Architects, Adelaide, SA. 4. **P:** Simon Kenny.

WORKING FURNITURE

Pg 110 1. **P:** Eric Victor-Perdraut. **A:** Bernard Penhey, Haysom Spender Architects, Brisbane, Qld. 2. **P:** Simon Kenny. **ID:** Burley Katon Halliday, Paddington, NSW.

Pg 111 3. **P:** Simon Griffiths. **ID:** Agatha Lim, Inter.Scape Design, South Yarra, Vic.

BATHROOM

Pg 112 **P:** Andre Martin. **A:** Michael Folk, Folk Lichtman & Associates, Waterloo, NSW.

BATHROOM ZONES

Pg 114 1. **P:** David Young. **ID:** Di Henshall, Hong Kong. 2. **P:** Simon Griffiths. **ID:** Agatha Lim, Inter.Scape Design, South Yarra, Vic.

Pg 115 3. **P:** Chris Bennett. **ID:** Melinda Boag Design, Yarralumla, ACT.

Pg 116 4. **P:** Simon Griffiths.

Pg 117 5. **P:** David Morcombe. **A:** Craig Steere Architects, Shenton Park, WA. 6. **P:** David Morcombe. **A:** Debra Brown, Hofman & Brown Architects, Cottesloe, WA.

BATHROOM STYLE

Pg 118 1. **P:** Dan Magree.

Pg 119 2. **P:** Dan Magree. **D:** David Hicks, Melbourne, Vic.

Pg 120 3. **P:** Eric Victor-Perdraut. **A:** Will Franklin, Noosaville, Qld.

Pg 121 4. **P:** Jeff Kilpatrick. **ID:** John Coote, Melbourne, Vic. 5. **P:** Rodney Weidland. **A:** Ken Charles, Centrum Architects, South Yarra, Vic.

Pg 122 6. **P:** Dan Magree. **A:** Nic Bochsler, Bochsler + Partners, Toorak, Vic. 7. **P:** Rob Frith. **A:** Ralph Drexel, Perth, WA.

Pg 123 8. **P:** Chris Groenhout. **ID:** John Coote, Melbourne. Vic.

BATHROOM COLOUR

Pg 124 1. **P:** Simon Kenny. **ID:** Meryl Hare, Hare + Klein, Woolloomooloo, NSW. 2. **P:** Simon Kenny.

Pg 125 3. **P:** Trevor Fox. **A:** Max Pritchard Architects, Kingston, SA. 4. **P:** Trevor Fox. **A:** Nic Bochsler, Bochsler & Partners, Toorak, Vic. 5. **P:** Andre Martin.

Pg 126 1. **P:** Dan Magree.

Pg 127 2. **P:** Dan Magree. 3. **P:** Andrew Elton. 4. **P:** Chris Bennett. 5. **P:** Dan Magree.

BATHROOM STORAGE

Pg 128 1. **P:** Dan Magree. **A:** Peter Maddison and Antony Di Mase, Maddison Architects, South Melbourne, Vic. 2. **P:** Eric Victor-Perdraut. **D:** Christiaan Stevens, Christiaan's, Wilton, Qld. 3. **P:** Eric Victor-Perdraut.

Pg 129 4. **P:** Simon Kenny. **A:** Bruce Townsend, Townsend & Associates Architects, O'Connor, ACT.

Pg 130 1. **P:** Simon Kenny. 2. **P:** Simon Griffiths. **ID:** Agatha Lim, Inter.Scape Design, South Yarra, Vic. 3. **P:** Andrew Payne. **A:** Kevin Snell Architects, Surry Hills, NSW. 4. **P:** Simon Kenny. **A:** Bruce Townsend, Townsend & Associates Architects, O'Connor, ACT. 5. **P:** Simon Griffiths. **ID:** Agatha Lim, Inter.Scape Design, South Yarra, Vic. 6. **P:** Ray Clarke. 7. **P:** Trevor Fox. **A:** Michael Pilkington and Susan Phillips, Phillips/ Pilkington Architects, Kensington, SA. 8. **P:** Greg McBean.

BATHROOM WALLS & FLOORS

Pg 132 1. **P:** Trevor Creighton.

Pg 133 2. **P:** Jeff Kilpatrick. **D:** Krisma Constructions, Sydenham, Vic.

Pg 134 1. **P:** David Morcombe. **A:** Richard Szklarz Architects, Cottesloe, WA. 2. **P:** David Morcombe. **A:** Richard Szklarz Architects, Cottesloe, WA. 3. **P:** Simon Kenny. **ID:** Concepts Interior Design, Deakin, ACT. 4. **P:** Jeff Kilpatrick. **A:** Bruce Katsipidis, Aktis, North Fitzroy, Vic. 5. **P:** Andrew Payne. **A:** David McCarroll, McMahons Point, NSW. 6. **P:** Greg McBean.

Pg 135 7. **P:** John Best. **ID:** Andrew Parr, Synman Justin Bialek, South Melbourne, Vic.

BATHROOM LIGHTING & WINDOWS

Pg 136 1. **P:** Eric Victor-Perdraut. **A:** Jeremy Salmon Architects, St Lucia, Qld.

Pg 137 2. **P:** Dan Magree. **ID:** Christine Saunders Design, Melbourne, Vic.

Pg 138 1. **P:** Russell Brooks. **A:** Leo Campbell, Campbell Luscombe Associates, Waterloo, NSW. 2. **P:** Simon Kenny. **A:** Urban Moo, Surry Hills, NSW. 3. **P:** Simon Kenny. **ID:** Meryl Hare, Hare + Klein, Woolloomooloo, NSW. 4. **P:** Simon Kenny. **A:** Leo Campbell, Campbell Luscombe Associates, Waterloo, NSW.

Pg 139 5. **P:** Russell Brooks. **ID:** Kathy Abbott, Tempo Interiors, Mosman, NSW.

Pg 140 1. **P:** Simon Kenny. **A:** Bruce Townsend & Associates, O'Connor, ACT. 2. **P:** Robert Frith. **A:** Paul Hofman, Hofman & Brown Architects, Cottesloe, WA.

Pg 141 3. **P:** Eric Victor-Perdraut. **A:** Will Franklin, Noosaville, Qld.

BATHROOM FIXTURES & FITTINGS

Pg 142 1. **P:** Eric Victor-Perdraut. **A:** Will Franklin, Noosaville, Qld.

Pg 143 2. **P:** Simon Kenny. **ID:** Meryl Hare and Dimity Haymen, Hare + Klein, Woolloomooloo, NSW.

Pg 144 1.&2. **P:** Robert Frith. **A:** Philip McAllister, Perth, WA. 3. **P:** Greg McBean. 4. **P:** David Young. **A:** John Gray, Archimages Architecture, Byron Bay, NSW. 5. **P:** Dean Wilmot. **A:** Michael Folk, Folk Lichtman Architects, Waterloo, NSW. 6. **P:** Greg McBean. 7. **P:** David Morcombe. **ID:** Anna Chandler, Cottesloe, WA. 8. **P:** Valerie Martin. 9. **P:** Dan Magree. **ID:** Christine Saunders Design, Melbourne, Vic.

Pg 146 1. **P:** David Morcombe. **A:** Craig Steere, Shenton Park, WA.

Pg 147 2. **P:** Jeff Kilpatrick. **A:** Steve Whiting, Whiting A&I, Albert Park, Vic. 3. **P:** David Morcombe. **A:** Debra Brown, Hofman & Brown Architects, Cottesloe, WA. 4. **P:** Dan Magree. **A:** Peter Maddison and Antony Di Mase, Maddison Architects, South Melbourne, Vic. 5. **P:** Chris Bennett. **ID:** Melinda Boag Design, Yarralumla, ACT.

BEDROOM

Pg 148 **P:** Andre Martin. **A:** Cox Richardson/Crone Associates, Sydney, NSW. **ID:** Idiom Design Practice & Cox Interiors, Sydney, NSW. Artwork: "Dandelion" digitally manipulated photograph by Rachel Fisha.

BEDROOM ZONES

Pg 1501. **P:** Simon Kenny. **A:** Brian Meyerson, Bondi, NSW. **ID:** Shellee Gordoun, Interiors with Zest, Moore Park, NSW. 2. **P:** Simon Kenny. **ID:** Concepts Interior Design, Deakin, ACT.

Pg 151 3. **P:** Simon Kenny. **ID:** Linda Kerry Design, Double Bay, NSW.

Pg 152 4. **P:** Eric Victor-Perdraut.

Pg 153 5. **P:** Eric Victor-Perdraut. **A:** Stephen Kidd Design and Fae Rentoul, Brisbane, Qld. 6. **P:** Russell Brooks. **ID:** Ruth Levine Designs, Paddington, NSW.

BEDROOM STYLE

Pg 154 1. **P:** Eric Victor-Perdraut. **A & ID:** Gabriel and Elizabeth Poole, Noosa, Qld.

Pg 155 2. **P:** Simon Kenny. **ID:** Leopa Design, Surry Hills, NSW.

Pg 156 3. **P:** Simon Kenny. **ID:** James Barbus and David Mathers, Daylesford, Vic.

Pg 157 4. **P:** Dan Magree. **ID:** Andrew Parr, Melbourne, Vic. 5. **P:** David Young.

Pg 158 6. **P:** Robert Frith. **ID:** Judith Barrett-Lennard, Perth, WA. 7. **P:** Simon Kenny. **ID:** Alexandra McKenzie, Elizabeth Bay, NSW.

Pg 159 8. **P:** Simon Kenny.

BEDROOM COLOUR

Pg 160 1. **P:** Simon Kenny. 2. **P:** Andre Martin. 3. **P:** Simon Kenny. **ID:** Urban Moo, Surry Hills, NSW.

Pg 161 4. **P:** Maree Homer. 5. **P:** Simon Kenny.

Pg 162 1. **P:** Elsa Hutton.

Pg 163 2. **P:** Maree Homer. 3. **P:** Andre Martin. 4. **P:** Maree Homer. 5. **P:** Maree Homer.

BEDROOM STORAGE

Pg 164 1. **P:** Simon Kenny. 2. **P:** Simon Kenny. 3. **P:** David Morcombe.

Pg 165 4. **P:** Dan Magree.

Pg 166 1. **P:** Oliver Ford. **A:** Andrew Macens, Macens Associates, Epping, NSW. 2. **P:** Chris Bennett. **ID:** Bridget Tyer, North Sydney, NSW. 3. **P:** Simon Kenny. **ID:** Jan Pollock and Dana Tosolini, Concepts Interior Design, Deakin, ACT. 4. **P:** Simon Kenny. **ID:** Urban Moo, Surry Hills, NSW. 5. **P:** Bill Anagrius. 6. **P:** Trevor Fox. 7. **P:** Dan Magree.

Pg 167 8. **P:** Simon Kenny. **ID:** Thomas Hamel, Woollahra, NSW.

BEDROOM WALLS & FLOORS

Pg 168 1. **P:** Simon Kenny.

Pg 169 2. **P:** Simon Kenny. **ID:** Pia Francesca Design, Moore Park, NSW. 3. **P:** Eric Victor-Perdraut. **A:** Paul Uhlmann Architects, Burleigh Heads, Qld. 4. **P:** Simon Kenny. **ID:** Nola Charles, Mascot, NSW. 5. **P:** Simon Kenny. **ID:** Michael Love Interior Design, Darling Point, NSW.

BEDROOM LIGHTING & WINDOWS

Pg 170 1. **P:** Dan Magree. **ID:** Andrew Mitchell, Urban Pad, Windsor, Vic.

Pg 171 2. **P:** Russell Brooks. **ID:** Richard Oddie, Paddington, NSW.

Pg 172 1. **P:** Dan Magree. **ID:** Jenny Goble, St Kilda, Vic. 2. **P:** Simon Kenny. 3. **P:** Dan Magree. **ID:** Danielle Trippett Interior Design & Decoration, Albert Park, Vic. 4. **P:** Jeff Kilpatrick. **A:** Steve Whiting, Whiting A&I, Albert Park, Vic.

Pg 173 5. **P:** Simon Griffiths. **D:** Mark Huntersmith, Ian James Smith Architects, East Melbourne, Vic.

BEDROOM FURNITURE

Pg 174 1. **P:** Bill Anagrius. 2. **P:** David Morcombe.

Pg 175 3. **P:** Bill Anagrius.

Pg 176 1. **P:** Simon Kenny.

Pg 177 2. **P:** Simon Kenny. **ID:** Meryl Hare, Hare + Klein, Woolloomooloo, NSW. 3. **P:** Dan Magree. **ID:** Fiona Austin, Stonehenge Interior Design, South Melbourne, Vic.

CHILDREN

Pg 178 **P:** Dan Magree. **ID:** David Mulhall, Accent On Design, Malvern, Vic.

CHILDREN ZONES

Pg 180 1. **P:** Elsa Hutton.

Pg 181 2. **P:** Simon Kenny. **ID:** Leroy Belle, Darlinghurst, NSW. 3. **P:** Simon Kenny. 4. **P:** Simon Kenny. **ID:** Karen Sarris, Canberra, ACT. 5. **P:** Chris Bennett. **ID:** Bridget Tyer, North Sydney, NSW.

CHILDREN COLOUR & DECORATION

Pg 182 1. **P:** Peter Clark. 2. **P:** Simon Kenny. **ID:** Linda Kerry, Double Bay, NSW. 3. **P:** Dan Magree.

Pg 183 4. **P:** Andre Martin.

Pg 184 1. **P:** Dan Magree.

Pg 185 2. **P:** Dan Magree. **ID:** Natalie Moss, Calamity Jane Interiors, Melbourne, Vic. 3. **P:** Simon Kenny. **ID:** Shellee Gordoun, Interiors with Zest, Moore Park, NSW. 4. **P:** Dan Magree. **ID:** Crowded House Design, Malvern, Vic. Artwork: "Purple Iris" painting by Elizabeth Tarrant. 5. **P:** Mark Green. **ID:** Hare + Klein, Woolloomooloo, NSW.

CHILDREN FURNITURE & STORAGE

Pg 186 1. **P:** Dan Magree.

Pg 187 2. **P:** Elsa Hutton. 3. **P:** Jeff Kilpatrick. 4. **P:** Mark Green. **ID:** Hare + Klein, Woolloomooloo, NSW. 5. **P:** Photo courtesy Designers Guild, London, UK. 6. **P:** Simon Kenny. 7. **P:** Andre Martin. 8. **P:** Mark Green. **ID:** Hare + Klein, Woolloomooloo, NSW.

index

Page numbers in *italics* refer to photographs

Editor-in-chief Anny Friis

Editor Rose-Marie Hillier   **Art director** Hieu Nguyen   **Copy editor** Jo McKinnon

Text Rose-Marie Hillier Jo McKinnon Julie Simpkin

Chief executive officer John Alexander
Group publisher Jill Baker
Publisher Sue Wannan
Editorial director Susan Tomnay

Produced by ACP Books
Printed by Dai Nippon Printing, Korea
Published by ACP Publishing Pty Limited, 54 Park Street, Sydney, NSW 2001 (GPO Box 4088, Sydney, NSW 1028),
phone (02) 9282 8618, fax (02) 9267 9438, acpbooks@acp.com.au and www.acpbooks.com.au
AUSTRALIA: Distributed by Network Services, GPO Box 4088, Sydney, NSW 1028,
phone (02) 9282 8777, fax (02) 9264 3278
UNITED KINGDOM: Distributed by Australian Consolidated Press (UK), Moulton Park Business Centre, Red House Road,
Moulton Park, Northampton, NN3 6AQ, phone (01604) 497 531, fax (01604) 497 533, acpukltd@aol.com
CANADA: Distributed by Whitecap Books Ltd, 351 Lynn Avenue, North Vancouver, BC, V7J 2C4, phone (604) 980 9852
NEW ZEALAND: Distributed by Netlink Distribution Company, Level 4, 23 Hargreaves Street,
College Hill, Auckland 1, phone (9) 302 7616

HOUSE.

Includes index.
ISBN 1 86396 285 9.
1. Interior decoration – Australia. I. Title: Australian House & Garden.

747.88

© ACP Publishing Pty Limited 2002
ABN 18 053 273 546
This publication is copyright. No part of it may be reproduced or transmitted in any form without the
written permission of the publishers. First published in 2002.

Front cover: Photography by Simon Kenny